Education in the 80's:

SPEECH COMMUNICATION

The Advisory Panel

Nobleza C. Asuncion-Lande, Associate Professor, Department of Speech and Drama, University of Kansas, Lawrence

Maridell Fryar, Coordinator of Fine Arts and Speech, Midland Independent School District, Texas

Patti P. Gillespie, Theater Department Head, University of South Carolina, Columbia

Jeff Golub, English Speech Teacher, Kent Junior High School, Washington

Thomas B. McClain, Chairman, Speech and Drama, New Trier East High School, Winnetka, Illinois

Carlene Elizabeth McDowell, Oral Communications and Language Arts teacher, Burnsville Senior High School, Minnesota

Anthony Mulac, Associate Professor and Vice Chairperson, Department of Speech, University of California, Santa Barbara

Education in the 80's:

SPEECH COMMUNICATION

Gustav W. Friedrich
Editor
University of Nebraska, Lincoln

Classroom Teacher Consultant
Joy H. McClintock
High School Speech Teacher
Seminole, Florida

National Education Association
Washington, D.C.

Stock No. 3165–2–00 (paper)
          3166–0–00 (cloth)

Note

The opinions expressed in this publication should not be construed as representing the policy or position of the National Education Association. Materials published as part of the NEA Education in the 80's series are intended to be discussion documents for teachers who are concerned with specialized interests of the profession.

Library of Congress Cataloging in Publication Data
Main entry under title:

Education in the 80's—speech communication.

  (Education in the 80's)
  Includes bibliographical references.
  1. Oral communication—Study and teaching—United
States.   I. Friedrich, Gustav W.   II. Series.
P95.4.U6E3   001.54'2'07073   80–24364
ISBN 0–8106–3166–0
ISBN 0–8106–3165–2 (pbk.)

Contents

Editor

Gustav W. Friedrich is Professor and Chair of the Department of Speech Communication at the University of Nebraska, Lincoln. He has co-authored *Teaching Speech Communication in the Secondary School* and *Growing Together . . . Classroom Communication.* Currently he is editor of *Communication Education* and President of the Central States Speech Association (1980–81).

Classroom Teacher Consultant

Joy H. McClintock teaches mass communication, public speech, and debate at Seminole Senior High School, Florida.

Review Board

The following educators acted as special consultants: Jan Andersen, Ronald E. Bassett, Samuel L. Becker, Edward M. Bodaken, William D. Brooks, Kenneth L. Brown, David E. Butt, Joseph N. Cappella, Peter Clark, Herman Cohen, Diana Corley, Sue DeWine, Raymond L. Falcione, Karen Garrison, Judy H. Goldberg, Paul H. Gray, Theodore G. Groves, Thomas A. Hollihan, Mary Frances Hopkins, Robert W. Hopper, F. Gerald Kline, Trevor Melia, Linda Moore, C. David Mortensen, Jody L. Nyquist, Edward J. Pappas, Malcolm R. Parks, Donna C. Sackett, Tulsi B. Saral, Robert L. Scott, Jo Sprague, David A. Thomas, Erika Vora, and Jane Work.

Not all speech communication classroom teachers are aware of the 1978 changes in the basic skills definition of Title II in the Elementary and Secondary Education Act of 1965. This 1978 legislative mandate not only identifies speaking and listening as basic skills but also calls upon both state and local agencies to reevaluate their speech communication programs and either restructure these programs or create new ones that place greater emphasis upon speaking and listening skills. The exact wording of Public Law 95-561 can be found on page 24.

With the inclusion of oral communication into the basic skills requirements, speech communication educators undertook the task of assessing and evaluating all phases of the speech communication curriculums. These findings indicate the majority of traditionally structured speech communication courses need more than minor modifications to meet the oral competency skill requirements of a large segment of our population.

In addition, student as well as school participation in traditionally structured extracurricular activities such as debate and forensics is declining. Rising transportation costs as well as student employment commitments on Saturdays and after school prohibit or severely limit student participation in these activities.

The classroom teacher, therefore, faces declining enrollment in basic course offerings, reduced participation in the traditional forms of extracurricular activities, and requests from school administrators to suggest ways to redesign programs and/or create new methods of providing the training necessary to help all who cross the threshold of the speech communication classroom to become competent oral communicators.

Within the pages of this book the classroom teacher will find guidelines, ideas, and proposals to lighten this seemingly insurmountable burden. Suggestions are offered to redesign the traditionally structured speech communication curriculums to provide the student with the communication competencies he or she needs to meet the challenges of the 1980's. In short, this book serves as an aid for the classroom teacher preparing personalized course outlines, determining functional competency levels, and planning new activities for the speech communication instruction of the 80's.

The directives are flexible because each communication course must be designed to meet the needs of the students of that specific community, as Roy Berko points out. Many of the authors stress the need for training in small group discussion, problem solving, decision making, group leadership, and interpersonal communication.

Andrew Wolvin believes that part of the career education training of the secondary student should be in effective speaking and listening to enter the job market with the necessary communication skills. As Cassandra Book reminds us, many students enter the job market directly from high school, and these students will benefit from special instruction in interpersonal skills as well as extending their communication skills through speaking and listening activities.

Paul Friedman's article on mainstreaming suggests the possibilities of extended group work and training in group leadership. He offers guidelines to help open communication lines between students in the mainstreamed classroom.

Peter Miller states that television is the only true mass medium and offers the mass communication teacher some excellent points to be considered when planning activities.

Regardless of the level of education, Miller feels the central task for all teachers is to instill in their students "a tolerance for opposing viewpoints" as well as "an appreciation for alternative cultural forms." The classroom teacher might be able to achieve these goals by offering students a wide variety of practical experiences in speaking and listening.

Of particular interest to the classroom teacher, then, are the suggestions of ways to extend the classroom instruction into the community, thus providing students with new opportunities to practice their communication skills. Although debate and forensics activities will continue to interest many students, James Klumpp reminds us that financial costs and limited time commitments of students will continue to be factors to consider in the 80's.

Most of the authors suggest ways the forensic and debate activities of the 70's can be expanded in the 80's to provide student participation in alternative activities that help them achieve oral communication competency. Cassandra Book suggests participation in speaking events through video-telephones as one answer to cutbacks in extracurricular activities. A modification of this is debating by cassette tape in much the same manner as chess is presently played by participants in various sections of the country.

Another possibility of extending the classroom instruction into the community is through the local radio station. Radio talk show hosts set up a premise or proposition at the opening of the program and open the phone lines to the public for questions and discussion with a panel of speech communication students.

Another variation of this utilization of local radio programming would be high school students debating local or national topics of interest in the locale. Radio listeners participate by calling in with their comments and registering their vote for the best debate team.

Learning experiences for students in the interpersonal or basic classes who wish to practice their communication skills can often be found within the teacher's own school system, as Lee Hudson and Beverly Whitaker Long note. Their ideas are sure to suggest other possible sources to the reader. One possibility that comes to mind is the social studies teacher. Presentations of mock student congresses by speech communication students give students in both disciplines the chance to practice their communication skills in nonthreatening situations.

One excellent way to develop and implement speech communication, theatre, and mass communication activities for the secondary student is through the speakers' bureau. Although many of the authors in this book either mention or allude to the value of a speakers' bureau, it is one form of alternative activity little used by classroom teachers in the 70's. The speakers' bureau concept can be as diverse in types of learning experiences and programs as teachers wish and students demand. Swing debates with local legislative representatives might draw large community crowds. Dramatizations of historical events have tremendous appeal for civic and community organizations.

As classroom teachers of speech communication redesign their curriculums and their instructional methods to train students in the communication skills needed in the real world beyond the classroom, the speech communication classroom of the 80's will become an exciting and stimulating place to be. As John Daly notes, there is no one correct way to teach.

Joy H. McClintock
Speech Teacher
Seminole High School
Seminole, Florida

It is especially refreshing to discover that a tone of optimism permeates the 20 chapters that comprise this document. I have grouped them in an order which, I hope, helps to focus on the overall concerns. In the first five chapters, the authors speculate positively about the future of speech communication instruction in five of its most common settings—elementary schools, secondary schools, community colleges, colleges and universities, and the world of work. Chapters 6 through 15 focus on an alphabetized arrangement of the major content areas for speech communication instruction as categorized by the National Center for Education Statistics. The remaining five chapters discuss instructional topics of special concern for speech communication teachers. Taken together, the 20 chapters provide many suggestions, predictions, alternatives, innovations, and improvements that can be either undertaken or accomplished during the 1980's. A careful reading of the chapters, then, should provide the speech communication teacher with creative responses to the bracing facts of the 80's.

Gustav W. Friedrich

CHAPTER 1

Speech Communication in the Elementary School

Barbara S. Wood
Content Consultants: David E. Butt
Pennsylvania State University
Robert W. Hopper
University of Texas at Austin

Education in the 1980's has begun with a new and exciting emphasis on basic skills in human development—and oral communication is now recognized as a critical skill in the educational process for children and youth. As a result of the passage of basic skills legislation, we will see speaking and listening included in the basic curriculum in our elementary schools. These dramatic changes will result:

1. The focus of language arts instruction will be broadened from the development of literacy skills (reading and writing) to the development of communication skills, including speaking and listening.

2. Teachers of language arts in the elementary schools will take a more functional approach, stressing practice in the types of communication each student needs to participate successfully in peer, family, and classroom relations.

3. Students will do more talking during instruction so that the classroom will be an alive, talkative, and sometimes chaotic environment.

This chapter outlines a speech communication program for elementary schools of the 80's. Instructional philosophy will begin to challenge an assumption that many teachers and parents have about children's language: Because children can talk, they are skilled in oral communication. Recent studies suggest that not only do children lack basic skills in oral communication but also they are often reticent to talk in front of others.[1] Their reticence stems from several sources, but one relates to classroom practices that emphasize nonoral modes of learning. If the goal of language arts instruction is to develop important, functional communication skills, then practice in effective speaking and listening must be emphasized in such programs. The programs that should be developed during the 80's are described in terms of four components: the content of instruction, the nature of the instructional process, techniques of classroom management, and instructional planning practices.

THE CONTENT OF THE PROGRAM

The content must include the most practical communication matters that apply to all people. While language patterns and particular communication forms vary from culture to culture and from situation to situation, communication functions are relevant to all of us, all of the time. This is why communication *functions* rather than *forms* should be emphasized. The following five functions should serve as the content:[2]

1. *Controlling:* Every day students deal with controlling situations, whether in the classroom or in the home. They seek to change the minds of others and react to others' pleas. They hope to affect the course of action on the playground and in their homes. Dealing with controlling requires practice in requesting, suggesting, refusing, and assenting, for example.

2. *Sharing feelings:* Some of the most important learning experiences involve sharing feelings with important people in our lives. While the understanding and sharing of our feelings have seldom been the focus of public school programs, future programs will benefit from these emphases. As a result, teachers must provide communication practice in praising, commiserating, expressing approval, apologizing, and responding to rejection.

3. *Informing:* Elementary language arts programs have always focused on clear expression of ideas. Refocusing instruction toward the oral dimension will necessitate some important

changes in order to include such communication strategies as explaining, naming, asking questions, and denying.

4. *Ritualizing:* When our messages help to sustain our social relationships, we are ritualizing, a communication strategy critical to building strong and healthy relationships with our family, friends, and teachers. Greeting, thanking, introducing, and teasing are exmples of this function.

5. *Imagining:* When we use language in ways that deal creatively with reality, we are imagining. To function successfully in the family, in the classroom, and with peers, students must develop such skills as speculating, fantasizing, and storytelling.

In the 1980's students will learn more about these five basic communication functions as teachers focus more on the practical skills necessary for effective speaking and listening. The shift from workbook activities and the written mode to encounter activities and oral learning should be an exciting one for elementary school students.

Four guidelines must be considered in adopting the functional communication approach in the classroom. First, communication is transactional. Our conversations with others involve a flow of ideas and feelings back and forth; no one is the speaker while the other is *only* the listener. Instead, both persons play both roles simultaneously; they listen and watch as they talk and move their bodies. Communication is not simply action + reaction—it is transaction.

A second guideline is that at any one time a communication situation almost always includes multiple functions; a person could be trying to change someone's mind (controlling) through rather personal means (sharing feelings). While one function might stand out as primary, multiple functions are typical of our everyday communications.

A third point about the content of instruction is that speech communication is really more than speech: Gestures, facial expressions, intonation patterns, and posture play significant roles in saying what we want to say to others. Further, we read the body language of others in such a way that, as some experts put it, the nonverbal communication we hear and see helps us to interpret the words we listen to.

Finally, anyone who is seriously considering alternate learning environments knows that one of the most effective ways of teaching students almost anything, from math and science to basic grammar, is through oral communication among teacher and students. An approach that sharpens oral communication skills will undoubtedly help students develop learning strategies in such other basic skill areas as, for example, mathematics.

THE INSTRUCTIONAL PROCESS

A model of competence presented by Connolly and Bruner has been selected as the instructional guide for the development of communication competence because it specifies the tasks essential to communication learning:[3]

1. Competence in any skill area must begin with the acquisition of an adequate *repertoire* of skills in that area. Speech communication teachers seek to develop in students an adequate and varied repertoire of communication strategies or acts that they can use effectively in important situations. Classroom instruction should be geared toward increasing the students' repertoires so that they have adequate alternatives in expressing affection, gaining someone's attention, asking for help when a task is too difficult, and assertively leading a group.[4]

2. Next, competence in any area requires the use of a set of *selection criteria* so that choices are appropriate. To achieve speech communication competence, students must learn the parameters defining the situation (participants, topic, task, and setting) so that they can adapt their messages to these parameters.[5] Further, conversational rules comprise selection criteria they must learn—e.g., stay on the topic, don't say too much, be truthful and have evidence, and be clear about what you say.[6]

3. The *implementation* of communication choices is the third component in the development of communication competence. Students must be given practice in the verbal and nonverbal strategies that might be appropriate for them in specific communication situations. Role playing and small-group discussion are important methods that the teacher can use to provide students with this practice. The environment of implementation must be supportive and helpful; the teacher must try not to be the prescriptive authority on the subject, but rather a moderator or discussion leader, trying to help students discuss and discover how they can communicate and how others respond to their attempts.

4. Finally, *evaluation* procedures must be clearly outlined for the teacher and the students. The teacher is not asked to present "the correct way"; rather, the students and the teacher discuss the appropriateness and effectiveness of alternative ways of accomplishing an objective. Personal objectives ("Did I say what I really meant?") and relational objectives ("Will he or

she still like me after I said that?") must be weighed. Students must consider what it means to adapt their communication to their partner.[7]

The four components of competence that outline the instructional process strongly suggest dramatic changes in the elementary school classroom. First, using this instructional process will undoubtedly change the classroom atmosphere. The increased use of role-playing and small-group instructional methods will mean a more modest role for the traditional "teacher talks, students listen" approach. As a result, the classroom may, at times, seem noisy and disorganized to the teacher who enjoys total control. My experience in working with teachers is, however, that the more they themselves are able to adapt to the model of instructional practice, the more comfortable they become with the new atmosphere.

CLASSROOM MANAGEMENT

Because the functional approach to language arts instruction is different from the approaches correlated with more traditional activities such as creative dramatics, puppetry, storytelling, and public speaking, it is essential that teachers adopt a new view of classroom management. Two critical management principles are at the heart of this view.[8]

One suggests that the teacher is the discussion leader, moderator, or facilitator for learning, not the prescriber of correct ways of communicating. As just discussed, elementary school teachers find it extremely difficult to adjust their teaching styles to the new functional communication approach. They worry that students will control the learning experience, they worry that things will get out of hand, and they "know" that nothing will be accomplished. For these teachers to gain experience in working within the guidelines of this approach (in, for example, in-service workshops) is essential. Also helpful to teachers who are trying this approach is a very carefully defined set of activities. Following small-group activities, for example, questions and answers define the analysis phase of instruction, in which the teacher is asked to refrain from giving specific suggestions (prescriptions). The use of small groups in order to include all students in the implementation will be difficult at first; teachers may worry that some groups will function effectively while others might not. But rather than concluding that a nonfunctioning group is a learning mishap, analyze aloud what took place in that group to gain valuable insight into the communication process.

17

The second factor in classroom management that sets this approach apart from more traditional ones is that virtually all of the students engage in implementation together. Students learn by doing, and much of the activity involves talking to each other; but an alive and rather noisy classroom atmosphere does not mean that learning cannot take place. Student involvement is the key to this approach, including participation in small-group activities and in follow-up classroom discussion. During the question–and–follow-up portion of instruction students will have to deal with important questions like these:

1. What different approaches did my friend try? (repertoire)

2. What reasons might have caused him or her to arrive at a decision to say this? (selection criteria)

3. Was he or she able to say what he or she wanted to say? Express what he or she wanted to? Did it seem to work for him or her? (implementation)

4. Was his or her approach more effective than another person's? Why? (evaluation)

During the question–and–follow-up portion of instruction, students will have to listen, watch, classify, comment, and support judgments about the communication in the classroom.

INSTRUCTIONAL PLANNING

Functional communication competencies develop outward—from classroom, to peer group, to family, and to the community. Students at all grade levels can benefit from instruction in the five basic communication functions, with differences in instruction resulting from the nature of the exercises and the expectations. Older, more experienced students will give more examples and will use both a larger repertoire of strategies and a more refined set of selection criteria. Further, they will probably be more skilled in implementing and evaluating their communication choices.

Because the functional communication approach is a recent development, there have been no large-scale applications of such programs. However, school districts and state education agencies in Ohio, Colorado, Pennsylvania, and Massachusetts, for example, have incorporated functional communication competencies into their curriculums. Districts and states interested in exploring these programs should contact these locations. Basic skills legislation mandates that educational agencies across the country teach oral communication—speaking and listening. Within the next few years, state education agencies will be able to provide information on model programs in functional communication.

The approach described here is practical and function-based, meaning that the *critical communication situations* worthy of study are not defined by theorists sitting in their offices. Instead, the skills to be developed are the products of real student needs as practical issues, human concerns, and important relationships become primary concerns. Probably the greatest strength of this approach is that, when done well, it is extremely sensitive to the needs of the students. Because of this, input from the students and their friends and families is essential; programs will, by definition, vary according to the type of community, the type of family life, and the type of communication demands. Everyday communication situations form the core of the learning experience so that students will gain the confidence and competence they need to succeed in their communication encounters.

If our instruction works well on the elementary level, and if secondary school programs continue to develop basic oral communication skills, then we can be confident that our public school graduates will be able to conduct themselves effectively during a job interview, ask for help when they need it, or express affection to a friend at that special moment. Our concerns about graduates (such as "Are they ready for the real world?") should be reduced as they participate in programs that are designed to develop their functional communication skills.

SUMMARY

Oral communication has finally been recognized as a basic educational skill. As a result, programs in the 1980's will focus on the essential functions of communication: controlling, sharing feelings, informing, ritualizing, and imagining. The purposes of instruction in speaking and listening will be to develop a repertoire of communication strategies for everyday communication, to develop a set of criteria for selecting from among these strategies, to develop ways of implementing communication choices, and to use criteria to evaluate communication attempts. Classroom management practices will shift from prescriptive and directive to analytical. Finally, instructional planning can be linked to new programs related to basic skills development in each state. The result for students? The classroom will become a more exciting place in which to communicate, to learn, and to develop effective speech communication skills.

REFERENCES

1. Garrison, John, and Garrison, Karen. "Measurement of Oral Communication Apprehension Among Children: A Factor in the Development of Basic Speech Skills." *Communication Education* 28: 119–128; 1979.

2. Wood, Barbara, editor. *Development of Functional Communication Competencies: Pre-K–Grade 6.* Urbana, Ill.: ERIC Clearinghouse on Reading and Communication Skills, 1977.

3. Connolly, Kevin, and Bruner, Jerome S. *The Growth of Competence.* New York: Academic Press, 1974. pp. 3–7.

4. White, Burton. "Critical Influences in the Origins of Competence." *Merrill-Palmer Quarterly* 21: 243–266; 1975.

5. Cazden, Courtney. *Child Language and Education.* New York: Holt, Rinehart and Winston, 1972. Also: "The Neglected Situation in Child Language Research and Education." *Language and Poverty: Perspectives on a Theme.* (Edited by F. Williams.) Chicago, Ill.: Academic Press, 1970. pp. 81–101.

6. Grice, H.P. "Logic and Conversation." *Syntax and Semantics: Speech Acts.* Vol. 3. (Edited by P. Cole and J. Morgan.) New York: Academic Press, 1975. pp. 41–58.

7. Delia, Jesse, and Clark, Ruth Anne. "Cognitive Complexity, Social Perception, and the Development of Listener-Adapted Communication in Six-, Eight-, Ten-, and Twelve-Year-Old Boys." *Communication Monographs* 44: 326–345; 1977. Also: "Cognitive Complexity, Social Perspective-Taking, and Functional Persuasive Skills in Second- to Ninth-Grade Children." *Human Communication Research* 3: 128–134; 1977.

8. In addition to the ERIC booklet already cited in reference 2, the "Additional Readings" that follow will provide valuable ideas for teachers.

Additional Readings

Allen, R.R., and Brown, Kenneth L., editors. *Developing Communication Competencies in Children.* Skokie, Ill.: National Textbook Co., 1976. This text reports the results of research in all phases of the development of functional communication. Instructional guidelines compatible with the present chapter's suggestions are offered.

Allen, R.R., and Wood, Barbara. "Beyond Reading and Writing to Communicative Competence." *Communication Education* 27: 286–292; 1978. This article outlines the functional communication approach, with special attention given to the relationship between literacy and oral communication.

Bassett, Ronald; Whittington, Nilwon; and Staton-Spicer, Ann. "The Basics in Speaking and Listening for High School Graduates: What Should Be Assessed?" *Communication Education* 27: 293–303; 1978. This article outlines in detail the communication competencies that the successful high school graduate should have acquired; though the title of this article suggests that concerns are only for secondary school students, elementary school educators can certainly draw implications for target behaviors and translate these competencies for their younger students.

Hopper, Robert, and Wrather, Nancy. "Teaching Functional Communication Skills in the Elementary Classroom." *Communication Education* 27: 316–321; 1978. Guidelines are presented to help classroom teachers develop worthwhile functional communication activities.

Larson, Carl. "Problems in Assessing Functional Communication." *Communication Education* 27: 304–309; 1978.

_____, and others. *Assessing Functional Communication.* Urbana, Ill.: ERIC Clearinghouse on Reading and Communication Skills, 1978. This booklet defines communication competence, discusses the dimensions of functional communication, and describes assessment procedures available today.

Wieman, John. "Needed Research and Training in Speaking and Listening Literacy." *Communication Education* 27: 310–315; 1978.

Wood, Barbara. *Children and Communication: Verbal and Nonverbal Language Development.* Part IV: "The Communication Situation." Second edition. Englewood Cliffs, N.J.: Prentice-Hall, Inc., 1981. This textbook follows the development of functional communication through the elementary school years and presents a series of communication competencies to be mastered during these years.

_____, editor. *Development of Functional Communication Competencies: Pre-K–Grade 6.* Urbana, Ill.: ERIC Clearinghouse on Reading and Communication Skills, 1977. Sample activities for pre-K through grade 6 students are given for the five communication functions; also, suggestions for classroom management are outlined.

CHAPTER 2

Speech Communication in the Secondary School

Cassandra L. Book
Content Consultants: Kathy Galvin
Northwestern University
Jody L. Nyquist
University of Washington

Although the adage "the only thing that is permanent is change" may have meaning elsewhere, it appears that secondary-level speech communication curriculums have undergone few modifications in recent decades. Indeed, the relatively unaltered, traditional speech offerings do not appear to reflect the legislative, societal, and career demands of the times; nor do they seem to fulfill the personal communication needs of the majority of our population. To help meet these needs and to provide students with communication competencies that will allow them to meet the challenges of a rapidly changing society, speech communication curriculums at the secondary level must undergo significant revision during the 1980's. In this chapter the author will describe the secondary speech communication curricular and extracurricular offerings of the late 1970's and then suggest ways in which speech communication courses can be responsive to the legislative, societal, career, and personal demands of the 1980's.

SPEECH COMMUNICATION IN THE LATE 1970'S

A survey of 15 states from coast to coast during the late 1970's[1] identified speech communication courses and/or programs in approximately 76 percent of the schools responding; approximately 24 percent indicated that no speech program was offered. Although the response rate varied from state to state, overall only 52 percent of the secondary-level schools responded to the questionnaire. Therefore, 76 percent is probably an overestimation of the percentage of schools overall offering speech (since schools with programs would be more likely to return the questionnaires than would those without programs).

The basic speech communication course was listed as elective in two-thirds of the schools and was required in only one-third of the schools. Thus, if 76 percent of the schools responding offered speech and, of those, only 33 percent required it, only 25 percent of the students were required to take a speech course.

The basic course was described as being one semester long and offered only once each year to a combination of ninth or tenth through twelfth graders. The average section had 20 students and was generally 55 minutes long. Although a combination of topics including interpersonal communication, discussion, oral interpretation, debate, and drama were usually taught in the basic course, public speaking dominated the course. The most frequently cited textbooks were *The Art of Speaking* by Elson and Peck (1966); *Basic Speech Experiences* by Carlisle (1969); *The New American Speech* by Hedde, Brigance, and Powell (1968); *Speaking of Communication* by Wilkinson (1975); *Person to Person* by Galvin and Book (1974); and *Patterns in Communication* by Hedde, Brigance, and Powell (1973). Evaluation of a combination of oral and written work was most common. Finally, 82 percent of the responding schools reported that speech was not combined with another course, but, when combined, it was most frequently taught with English.

Beyond the basic course, the rank order of advanced courses overall and the mean percentages of schools offering them were as follows: (1) drama, 59.5 percent; (2) advanced speech, 30.3 percent; (3) debate, 26.5 percent; (4) radio/television/mass media, 18.5 percent; (5) oral interpretation, 14.9 percent; (6) film, 11.2 percent; (7) discussion, 7.6 percent; and (8) interpersonal communication, 7 percent.

Of the extracurricular offerings, theatre or drama was the most popular with an average of 78.2 percent of the schools offering it. Forensics (individual events) was offered by a mean of 53.5 percent of the schools, debate by 39.6 percent, and discussion or student congress by 17.5 percent. Other activities such as speakers' bureaus and competitive speaking for community service group awards and scholarships were also mentioned.

The responses revealed little change in terms of basic or advanced course offerings in the states where comparisons were made with studies completed in the previous 10 years. Since the discipline of speech communication has undergone significant modification during the 1970's, it appears particularly appropriate that speech communication educators devote themselves to revising their secondary curriculums to meet the needs and demands of the 1980's.

DEMANDS OF THE 1980'S ON THE CONTENT OF SPEECH COMMUNICATION COURSES

Legislative Demands

The very fact that speech communication has now become a basic skill by law should be reflected in *what* is taught and *how* it is taught. Title II of the Elementary and Secondary Education Act of 1965 was amended in the new Title II, which was adopted on November 1, 1978, to read as follows:

> The purpose of this part is—(1) to assist Federal, State and local educational agencies to coordinate the utilization of all available resources for elementary and secondary education to improve instruction so that all children are able to master the basic skills of reading, mathematics, and effective communication, both written and oral; (2) to encourage States to develop comprehensive and systematic plans for improving achievement in the basic skills; (3) to provide financial assistance to State and local educational agencies for the development of programs in the basic skills. . . . (Public Law 95-561)

The inclusion of speaking and listening as basic skills puts new demands on schools to identify ways in which this legislative mandate for speech instruction is being met or to create units or courses to satisfy this requirement. From the research cited above, it appears that many schools will have to add courses in speech or will have to demonstrate how instruction in speaking and listening skills is integrated into their language arts curriculums. In addition, speech courses (or at least units) will have to be required rather than elective, and means of assessing students' speaking and listening skills will have to be created and implemented.

To be in compliance with the legislation, students will have to be instructed in speaking and listening, not merely asked to speak and listen as part of another exercise. Hopefully, as a result of Title II, educators will not be allowed to say that students who simply give oral reports to their peers, for example, are receiving actual instruction in improving their speaking and listening skills. Specific instruction designed to improve students' abilities to use the five communication functions—informing, controlling, sharing feelings, ritualizing, and imagining—must be provided, and the students' abilities in these areas must be assessed.[2] As indicated in Chapter 1 by Barbara Wood, these functions should become the basis for the design of curriculums and the creation of instructional objectives.

Thus, the legislation of the 70's and 80's has placed new demands on the curriculum that potentially will bring as much attention to speaking and listening as to the other basic skills of reading, writing, and arithmetic.

Societal Demands

A second major demand of the 80's results from our society's need for articulate speakers who can provide effective leadership, problem solving, and decision making within groups, organizations, and government. Since speech communication has a long history of research and teaching in these areas, it should be simple to develop courses that provide students with opportunities to work through problem-solving procedures as they tackle meaningful issues, particularly those upon which students can have an impact. Students need to learn to consider problems and the myriad of contributing issues from various points of view, and to reach decisions through systematic analysis of the advantages and disadvantages of each potential solution. They need to experience firsthand the complexities of bringing about change in a highly integrated world so that they (1) can empathize more with the public officials and other managers who make policy decisions and solve problems that affect them, (2) can make more meaningful and informed contributions to policy changes, when possible, and (3) can have an effective impact on a particular system, when necessary, by organizing appropriate communication strategies.

Group problem-solving activities that involve effective use of all the functions of communication should be helpful in training students to provide leadership or simply to participate more effectively in the American democratic process and on various task forces and committees of communities and companies. High school students who experience this group problem-solving process should be prepared, as adults, to better solve problems, make decisions, and articulate both the solutions and the reasons supporting these solutions. While teachers in many disciplines work toward these goals, the complex communication aspects of these activities should be handled by a communication specialist at the secondary level.

The energy, economic, and sociological problems of the 80's promise only to be more complex than in the past and to penetrate all social strata of the country. The late 1960's and early 1970's was a time of violent response to problems that left most people dissatisfied with protest demonstrations, rock throwing, and bra burning as solutions to problems or as means of effective and permanent change. Hopefully, with improved and more widespread training of secondary school students in the effective use of communication to research and articulate problems and solutions, the Americans of the next decades will reap the benefits of effective solutions, thoughtful decisions, and good leadership.

The communication courses of the 1980's must make students more intelligent and critical consumers of the media, particularly given the fact that for the typical adult, media consumption is a major activity for at least three and one-half to four hours per day. The behavioral, cognitive, and affective influences of the media are evident.[3] As a result, students must be made aware of the impact of the media on their understanding of the world conditions, voting and purchasing behavior, life-styles, etc., and should be encouraged to consider alternative ways of fulfilling their leisure time rather than being passive receptacles of the media messages. They should be encouraged to devote more time to activities that include communicating with other people in interpersonal, small-group, and public settings. In addition, students must be taught to be effective creators of mass media. Since media technology is available at increasingly low cost, the traditional consumer will have more chance to enjoy videotape, film, and even public broadcast. Thus, the communication course might add to the students' abilities to critically consume the media by giving them "hands-on" experience in producing media messages.

Career Demands

A third major demand of the 80's is created by the reality of frequent career changes: Individuals need a variety of communication skills that will help them secure and maintain jobs. As a result of today's rapidly changing world, the increased use of technology that makes some jobs obsolete, and the personal desire for growth and change, the average individual will, after college graduation, make three significant career changes and hold approximately nine jobs. Thus, students going into the job market need practice in interviewing and in verbally packaging their skills, aspirations, and personal characteristics in ways that are best suited to their prospective employers' job needs. Communication skills are critical not only in interviewing for the job but also in keeping the job. Research on the 1979–80 trends in the recruiting of college graduates indicated that "companies rated competent writing and speaking skills tops among the qualities sought in prospective employees."[4] Interpersonal skills were also frequently rated as necessary.[5] Since employers indicate that these skills are necessary for the success of college graduates in the interview and, consequently, on the job, high school students may find them necessary as well, depending upon the job. Faced with a future that promises frequent job changes, students need special preparation in interviewing, public and interpersonal communication, and writing skills that will allow them versatility in adapting to the range of career communication they are likely to experience.

Personal Communication Demands

The fourth, and perhaps most significant, demand of the 80's is for the fulfillment of personal communication needs. In a highly "future-shocked" world characterized by transience, increased leisure time, pervasive technology, lack of permanent friendships, unstable family units, information bombardment, and media hype, individuals need improved communication skills so that they can cope with and act on, not merely react to, the stimuli. While educators in many disciplines will attempt to help people to cope with contemporary life, the work of the speech communication teacher in fostering effective communication becomes more and more critical as the sheer frequency of interaction (both machine and interpersonal) increases.

Students in the 80's need to recognize that they are not effective communicators merely because they talk "naturally" and frequently. They need to be made conscious of their communicative incompetence and then be provided with a model for assessing and systematically improving their communication skills.[6] Students need to increase their repertoire of verbal means of informing, controlling, sharing feelings, ritualizing, and imagining. They need to learn to carefully consider which communication behaviors they choose based on the participant, situation, timing of the message, purpose, etc. They need to be able to implement the communication choices they make and, finally, to evaluate the success or failure of their messages based on the receivers' verbal and nonverbal responses. If students are trained to consider this model when making, implementing, and evaluating their communication choices, they should become not only more competent communicators but also more responsible communicators who recognize and accept

27

responsibility for the powerfulness of their talk. Such improved communication competency and responsibility could have a positive impact on all types of personal relationships from employee–employer to intimate and family interactions.

Since self-concepts are gained through interaction with others, learning to give and receive personal feedback is valuable. Use of open and honest, yet supportive, communication is a skill to be gained through practice in interpersonal communication classes. In addition, learning to express feelings and empathize with others, to listen for content as well as emotional responses, and to make responsible and congruent choices in verbal and nonverbal expressions are communication skills that potentially could help people to overcome the breakdown of interpersonal relationships. Similarly, skills in conflict management and in building relationships with those "selected others" by sharing various levels of information (including self-disclosure) and by relating to people as individuals, not merely as roles, should be emphasized in secondary-level speech communication courses so that students can better cope with the daily pressures that pull people apart.

Educators must also create opportunities for students to participate in extracurricular speaking events that add to their communication competence, increase their self-confidence and self-concepts, and provide opportunities to receive feedback on their communication skills. Gasoline and energy shortages and budgetary cutbacks have decreased the feasibility of students' traveling great distances to participate in extracurricular activities. However, new technological developments such as video-telephones may eventually be used so that students from distant parts of the country can debate. More intraschool and local school district programs may have to be created or expanded. Regardless of the method, extracurricular speech activities should be maintained to allow additional experiences for students who seek them.

SUMMARY

Title II requires that instruction in speaking and listening be made available for all students in the 1980's. The energy, economic, and sociological problems of the 80's, as well as increased media bombardment, will make it even more necessary to develop students' problem-solving skills through speech communication instruction. To help individuals secure and maintain jobs in an era of frequent job and career changes, communication courses will need to provide practice in functional communication skills. Finally, to help people cope with the "future-shocked" world of the 80's, communication courses will need to focus on the fulfillment of personal communication needs. Thus, because communication needs are reflected in our legislation, society, careers, and personal lives, we must do all that we can to increase the communication competence of the secondary-level students who are on the threshold of creating our future.

REFERENCES

1. Data gathered by independent researchers using the same basic questionnaire in Maryland, Massachusetts, Pennsylvania, Kentucky, Georgia, Texas, Minnesota, Wisconsin, Michigan, Ohio, Indiana, Nebraska, Oklahoma, North Dakota, and Washington will be reported in a forthcoming article by Cassandra L. Book and Edward J. Pappas.

2. The functional communication competencies are described in the following:

Allen, R.R., and Brown, Kenneth, editors. *Developing Communication Competence in Children.* Skokie, Ill.: National Textbook Co., 1976.

Wood, Barbara Sundene. *Development of Functional Communication Competencies K–6 and 7–12.* Falls Church, Va.: Speech Communication Association, 1977.

Book, Cassandra. "Teaching Functional Communication Skills in the Secondary Classroom." *Communication Education* 27, November 1978.

Hopper, Robert, and Wrather, Nancy. "Teaching Functional Communication Skills in the Elementary Classroom." *Communication Education* 27, November 1978.

3. Atkin, Charles A., and Greenberg, Bradley S. "The Effects of the Mass Media." *Human Communication: Principles, Contexts, and Skills.* (Edited by Cassandra L. Book.) New York: St. Martin's Press, 1980. pp. 194–224.

4. "College Grads to Find '80 Job Hunting Easier." *The Detroit News,* December 9, 1979. p. 14-B.

5. Shingleton, John D., and Scheetz, L. Patrick. *Recruiting Trends 1979–80: A Study of Businesses, Industries, Governmental Agencies, and Educational Institutions Employing New College Graduates.* East Lansing: Michigan State University Placement Services, 1979. pp. ii–iii.

6. The competency model can be found in the sources listed in reference 2 above.

CHAPTER 3

Speech Communication—
A Community College Perspective

Roy M. Berko
Content Consultants: Diana Corley
Black Hawk College
Judy H. Goldberg
Arapahoe Community College

Community colleges are unique on the American education scene. While many four-year schools are out searching for students, and others are seeing a drop, or even a leveling-off, in enrollments, community colleges continue to grow. Even as secondary-school populations decline, community colleges are expanding by drawing on populations other than recent high school graduates.

Why is this phenomenon currently taking place? What is unique about the community college that allows for a trend other than the norm? What about the future? It is the purpose of this chapter to explain the author's feelings and observations on this phenomenon as it relates to speech communication programs at community colleges in the 1980's.

Community colleges find themselves in a unique educational position because they have low tuition rates; offer college-parallel (the first two years of the traditional four-year college or university program) as well as technical programs; are located in areas where individuals can work and attend school; and offer special interest and noncredit courses. There appears to be no reason to believe that the trend will change. In fact, if anything, there should be expanded growth.

Besides the traditional, just-out-of-high-school students, post-secondary institutions are drawing new types of students: (1) women who wish to be trained to enter the job market due to economic conditions, the growth of female independence, or the desire for a change in life-style; (2) individuals who need new training or advanced training based on new techniques as a knowledge of computers becomes necessary in an increasing number of occupations, as technologically sophisticated equipment replaces semi-skilled workers, and as new licensing requirements (involving certification for those seeking real estate and health careers, for example, and for paraprofessionals in various fields) are enacted; (3) early retirees who are looking for another career; (4) individuals from lower socioeconomic groups who seek upward mobility; (5) minorities who feel they now might have a chance to enter the job market; (6) foreign students; and (7) newly immigrated individuals.

The population of potential community college students appears to be ever-expanding. What effect will this have on community college speech programs?

1. Most community colleges are open-door institutions (because there are no academic restrictions, any student can enter). As a result, many students coming to these institutions are ill-equipped to handle the oral and listening requirements of academic life. It would seem, therefore, that many will need course work below the basic course offering. Fortunately, the number of developmental courses is on the upswing. As an example, programs are being developed based on the excellent work of Barbara Strain and Pat Wysong (San Antonio Community College) and supplemented by that of Maria Miller (Jefferson Community College, Louisville, Kentucky) and Fran Bostwick, Barbara Finegan, and Roy Berko (Lorain County Community College, Elyria, Ohio). Realistically, most urban colleges and many rural community colleges must accept responsibility for the fact that they are enrolling students who simply cannot "cut it" and will drop out, or who will never reach their potential because the colleges do not offer the developmental, remedial, or supplemental training that these students must have.

2. Noncredit courses must be developed to supplement the academic offerings. As more people have increased leisure time, there is a need to fill those hours. Such offerings as a practicum in humanities (allowing students to attend plays, musicals, or concerts, and then discuss them); dramatic productions that allow for community participation; interpersonal communications courses; workshops in such topical areas as self-

31

awareness, assertiveness training, and attitude assessment; and public speaking classes can be developed for students not interested in receiving credit, but wishing to fill in their time with meaningful activities.

3. Programs must also be developed to meet the needs of specific groups within the community. Community colleges should work with local businesses, industries, hospitals, and social service institutions in training their people in specific communication skills: group discussion, leadership, public speaking, stress communication, and nonverbal communication. All of these courses would be geared to a particular group and presented either on the college campus or on-site at the organization.

4. A realistic evaluation must be made of the types of skills that students need in social and career settings. Community colleges should examine the field of communication and ascertain exactly which skills their students are going to need to be successful in a collegiate atmosphere, in the world of work, and in the various types of personal relationships they will form. The speech program, and especially the basic course (which is, unfortunately, the only communication course most students take), should then be designed to reflect these needs. It is my belief that many instructors who are being influenced by the "back to basics" movement are mistakenly interpreting this to mean a return to public speaking, exclusively. It is my opinion that students need a balanced program that will teach them how to structure communicative messages (whether for a public speech or for an interpersonal interaction), improve their listening skills, introduce them to interpersonal communications concepts (relationship development and endings), give them a general knowledge of the operation of the group process, and provide them with new understanding of the language we use (in both verbal and nonverbal contexts). Such a program will at least give students the basis for building an understanding of the communicative act and the contexts in which they have been, and will be, operating.

5. Because of their close ties to the area in which they are located, more and more two-year-college instructors of speech communication should become involved in community-based consulting. This can and will happen only if the faculty members let it be known that they have such expertise and then actively

32

pursue consulting opportunities. Presently, *the* word is COM-MUNICATIONS. Two-year-college instructors can do themselves and their communities a great service by helping others—in such settings as industry, health career agencies, and social service agencies, for example—become more effective communicators.

6. A study conducted by the author revealed that of 250 community colleges surveyed, only 36 percent offered a two-year degree program in communications, with 10.2 percent offering a two-year technical degree program. Specific, speech-oriented two-year programs included course work in multimedia communication, broadcasting, applied theatre arts, broadcast engineering technology, visual arts, theatre arts, and speech communication.

   At an Action Caucus held at the Speech Communication Association (SCA) convention in 1977, it was revealed that several institutions were proposing degree programs in sign language. Such programs have now been developed and appear to be providing a much-needed service in the communities in which the sponsoring colleges are located.

   An effort should be made by SCA and the Community College Section of SCA (1) to ascertain what types of speech programs should be developed that would fit into a two-year time allocation and (2) to develop curriculums that would implement these programs.

7. Community colleges tend to be conservative in their course offerings. Surveys indicate that most offer a single basic course in speech communication, although some offer an additional course in interpersonal communication or specialized communication—e.g., Business and Organizational Speaking, Speech for Technicians, Speech for Nurses, Interviewing, Interpersonal Communications for Health Careers.

   The more courses that are offered, the more interest grows in the entire field, and the more demand there is for additional courses and additional sections. Though this expansion should take place, we cannot realistically assume that community colleges, as a whole, are going to greatly expand their offerings unless the newly emerging trend to offer specific courses for specific people becomes a more dynamic movement.

8. Community colleges are, and will continue to be, the institutions called upon to socialize America's newcomers. Whether

these people are the newly immigrated or the foreign students who come for further training, they have the same need—to improve their communication skills. Two-year institutions are experiencing a greater demand for courses such as English as a Second Language.

9. As more and more states pass legislation to ensure education in the basic skills, there will be a need for more skill training in communications. Concomitantly, there will be a need to focus on basic speech competencies and to ensure that each student, after having taken a speech course, will have at least the minimum competence required to communicate in the marketplace.

10. The persons best qualified to save our cities in the 80's will be those who will be able to work against the grain of increased alienation. Individuals trained in speech communication will be better equipped than most to mediate differences, to act as conflict managers. Ideally these professionals would come from community college staffs because the instructors are known to, and familiar with, the community.

11. A serious problem confronting community college communication programs is the quality and type of instructors teaching at these institutions. With the present Ph.D. glut, many graduates who possess a doctorate degree are pursuing community college positions. While these professionals are often well versed in research and scholarship, community colleges need *trained teachers,* a skill often overlooked in many doctorate programs. A university and a community college are separate entities, and speech communication faculties have unique thrusts in each type of institution. One of the challenges that community colleges will have to meet during the 80's is the strong verbalization of the separate but equal concept in professional preparation for its future faculty members.

Community colleges are unique institutions, and because of this, the speech communication programs within these institutions can do much to reach out and serve the various factions within the communities in which they are located. They are already doing this in many places, but with special effort, even more can and will be accomplished.

CHAPTER 4

Speech Communication
As the New Humanities

Roderick P. Hart
Content Consultants: Samuel L. Becker
University of Iowa
Herman Cohen
Pennsylvania State University

A PREAMBLE

Before proceeding further, the reader should be warned that he or she is about to read a polemic. Although polemical writing is the discourteous cousin of the academic essay, it has an honorable history in the more turbulent realm of political and social affairs. Normally, the polemic has two rhetorical features: (1) it is more negative than the facts warrant, and (2) it overstates the case that it attempts to make. If the polemic has such disreputable features, why use it? I state my case polemically because certain trends in higher education disturb me, because I feel that these trends deserve discussion, and because I do not have a ready solution to the problems that attend them. Naturally, if these problems were easily solved, I would have cast my remarks in a less disputatious and more courtly style.

In the other chapters of this book, positively stated and rationally deliberated goals for the field of speech communication are presented to the reader. If my essay, thus, constitutes the lunatic fringe of this volume, it is because I feel that no set of purely "academic" goals can be reached until the psychological environment surrounding the teaching profession is taken into consideration as well. I have chosen the polemical form because queries raised in a vigorous fashion are likely to be noticed. Although I beg the reader's forgiveness for sailing this essay between the Scylla of the Impolitic and the Charybdis of the Impolite, I do not apologize for the questions raised because they can steer us truly.

Be aware. The heathens are among us. Oh, I suppose that they have always been among us. A nation could hardly have listened to the mindless cant of the 60's or watched the even more tedious situation comedies of the 70's without producing a heathen or two. But the 1980's threaten to deify a new kind of heathen, a person I choose to call the New Philistine.

The New Philistines are becoming well ensconced in all areas of endeavor. They have raised to the heights the corporate director of General Motors and dashed underfoot the Peace Corps volunteer; they have nurtured a shocking illiteracy in the United States, while at the same time causing the circulation of the *National Inquirer* to soar; and they have produced the overpaid athlete, the TV dinner, the Watergate ethic, and the white flight mentality. The New Philistines have done their best to sap creativity from popular entertainment, to substitute barbarism for political morality, and to replace precious energy resources with homilies from the major oil corporations.

I suppose that indignities such as these should give us all pause. But our real call to arms has only recently been sounded. The New Philistines have screwed up their courage sufficiently to take on higher education itself. They have introduced into academia the administration's FTE ratio, the faculty's labor union, and the library's mutilated copy of *Time* magazine. They have smiled approvingly upon the social scientist's multiple-choice examination, the Business School's Chair of Free Enterprise, and the English Department's desperate foray into popular culture. They have helped to create (and reward) the one-day-on-campus entrepreneurial professor, the afternoon soap opera break in student dormitories, and the meretricious second administrative assistant to the Vice-Provost.

This metaphor of the New Philistine is not simply a catch-all device useful for launching an attack on sundry ills. Nor are these people imaginary. The New Philistines stalk the college campus and must be resisted. In these remarks I shall offer explanations for the rise of the New Philistines and suggest attitudes that may prove useful to those of us in speech communication who wish to resist their blandishments. Although I may be blinded by the privations of the times, I doubt that teachers of speech communication could perform a more important service than that of dispatching the New Philistines in this, the eleventh, hour.

Definitionally, the New Philistinism in higher education is the acolyte of the cost-efficient, academic quick fix. Mixed metaphor run amok? Not completely. The theological, economic, and pharmacological images help to point up the tremendous influence of the New Philistines. Above all, they are True Believers. They preach the doctrine of positivism, arguing that society's problems are essentially technological in nature and, therefore, require essentially technological palliatives. The New Philistines also come garbed as academic capitalists who hold that market demands should determine all educational priorities, all curricular development, and all faculty recruitment. Perhaps because they have, thus, combined ersatz religion with short-sighted economics, the academic Philistines find their peak experiences to be chemical rather than transcendental in nature. When a New Philistine describes an educational institution to a television audience between halves of a Saturday afternoon football game, he or she makes orgiastic allusions to its famed nuclear accelerator, to its lengthening cadre of law school graduates, to its burgeoning enrollment in data processing, and to its newly developed technique for increasing hog production. Rarely these days do we find academic institutions described as legitimate havens for those who love literature, music, or art; who want to know something of their cultural heritage; or who wish to detect moral dilemmas *before* the special prosecutor knocks on their doors.

All of this nay-saying of mine may seem untoward for one who was born at the height of America's technological development, who was educated at land-grant institutions, and who does his professing in that pragmatic liberal art (or applied social science) called speech communication. Indeed, when the academic founders of speech communication left their scholarly colleagues in English because of the latter's reluctance to teach communication skills, they did so because they sought to transmit practical knowledge; to help their students make a difference in the corporate, legal, and religious circles of the early twentieth century. Speech communication began as a pragmatic discipline, and it hopefully will remain one. Most of us in speech communication continue to echo James Winans' desire to devote our classes to making people more useful when they talk.

To acknowledge that the roots of speech communication are practical is not to say that our discipline should become first handmaiden to the New Philistines. But the danger of this happening has never been greater. For perhaps the first time in the twentieth century, enrollment trends in higher education are heavily favoring speech communication.

One need not meander far at a professional convention to overhear tales of burgeoning enrollments being swapped by beleaguered faculty members in our departments. Professors of environmental science are increasingly advising their students to improve their communication skills (perhaps because the politics of energy presents such intricate rhetorical problems for its spokespersons). As enrollments in schools of business continue to soar, courses in interviewing, group discussion, and organizational communication are seen—rightly or wrongly—as attractive adjuncts to curricular offerings in management, marketing, and finance. Courses in speech communication have long been attractive to pre-law majors, as well as to persons headed for the ministry. With those professions becoming more popular; with other "boom" areas like nursing, policy studies, and engineering making demands upon us; and with cognate areas like journalism and radio–television–film finding that we are adept at helping people to become articulate, we in speech communication will find ourselves in the academic catbird seat all too quickly.

Or will we? What adaptations are required of us when students arrive in our classes from departments of civil and mechanical engineering rather than from departments of history, English, and philosophy? What special burdens are placed upon us when we teach students who have never mastered a foreign language (and, hence, have never learned certain elementary principles of audience adaptation), who have limited abilities to commit their thoughts to paper, or who are unable to sustain an argument beyond the level of moral expediency? Although the New Philistinism may well have filled our departmental coffers, its munificence costs us something. Because they spring from a sharply intensified and unthinking cultural pragmatism, the economics of college enrollments threaten to sully us as an academic discipline. Unless we as teachers of speech communication take certain steps to counteract the New Philistinism, it will engulf us.

There are signs that the barbarians may already be at hand. Some of our basic textbooks, for example, are still too reductionistic. Replete with staccato-like prose and glossy photos of people chatting on a park bench, these textbooks tell us that the principles of effective communication can be reduced to formula. We are told definitively that "research has shown that a two-sided approach to speech organization is best." We are asked to learn by rote the "ten principles of effective speech delivery." We are invited to work our minds around a gaggle of end-of-chapter exercises suitable, perhaps, for prepubescents. The oftentimes painfully human side of communication is skirted in such textbooks. The educated guesswork that is our sole guide to effective human interaction is given short shrift. The artistry and—yes, damn it—the essential *mystery* of how human beings come to share ideas and feelings are lost amidst a barrage of half-truths and pap. Some textbook publishers now seem to be telling their authors that since the college sophomore can read only at the eleventh-grade level, they (the authors) are justified in thinking their thoughts at that level.

We might excuse such textbook authors for their transgressions since they have little choice but to dance to the tune of the corporate Philistines who publish the books they write. And, perhaps, it is not entirely fair to indict those college faculty members who find it wise these days to peddle communicative bromides to the Young Philistines who demand the sort of "bottom-line" knowledge they receive in their accounting classes. But surely someone must be blamed for students who appear to believe that the process of communication is merely a concatenation of variables interacting deterministically to produce a set of results. Someone must be held accountable for those students who think that mastering the rules of parliamentary procedure will *alone* produce an essential sort of wisdom. Someone must explain why college debaters sometimes sound like mannequins spewing forth verbiage at a pace lagging just behind that of the speed of light. Someone must be made to defend the proliferation of classes that operate under the sobriquet of "relevant, experientially based, nonverbal encounters" and that have as their sole legitimate function the dramatization of the longevity of classical forms of sophistry. Someone *must* atone for these sins against the human spirit.

But it profits us little to seek out the perpetrators of such crimes. We should turn ourselves to seeking remedies and to battling the New Philistinism in all of its many contemporary forms. It would be a mark of disciplinary maturity to do so, it would be strategically advantageous on campus to do so, and, most important, it would be to our students' benefit to do so.

At the very least, college teachers of speech communication should remind themselves of certain principles upon which the discipline is based. To wit:

1. *Human communication is a human phenomenon.* Because it is human, communication operates in the realm of the contingent, it is not reducible to a set of scholastic maneuvers, and it is never completely divorced from the realm of the moral.

2. *Human communication is a behavioral phenomenon.* When we talk, we do so obviously. To engage in communication is to become involved in a mind–body process of dynamic contact with a living, breathing Other.

3. *Human communication is a practical phenomenon.* Speech gets the work of the world done. Normally, it is neither pretty not effete. Its cultural effects are typically unspectacular; its effects upon us as individuals are oftentimes painfully noticeable.

Perhaps I should apologize for offering this rather traditional litany to college teachers of speech communication. But in the heady atmosphere of high enrollments (or in the less glorified one of searching for a sufficient number of students' bodies to fill our classes), it becomes easy to forget who we are and where we must go. My thesis is a simple one: Speech communication must become the New Humanities. This is not to say that the traditional disciplines in the liberal arts will, perforce, fold up their tents and quit the academic scene. It is to suggest, however, that as long as our students minimize their contacts with literature, history, art, and ethics—and take courses in speech communication in their stead—we as a discipline have a special obligation to preserve and nourish traditional academic values.

This charge is not nearly as awesome as it may seem. When students take a beginning course in speech communication, they are already being asked to think in a humanistic way, in a rhetorical way. To think rhetorically means, at the very least, to think about the resources of language as well as to learn how to utter words. To think rhetorically means to consider the cultural assumptions of would-be listeners and to take those assumptions into account when speaking to them. To think rhetorically means to acknowledge that all ideas—even technological ones—are debatable ideas and that no idea has pre-eminence unless people grant it the same. To think *well* rhetorically is to seize upon the ethical dimensions of a human issue and to lay them bare for listeners. To think *well* rhetorically is to reason consecutively, to structure ideas and arguments in ways understandable to persons ignorant of those ideas and arguments. To think *well* rhetorically is to disbelieve almost everything one hears and to take intellectual solace in that skepticism.

Implicitly, perhaps, the best speech communication courses have always taught these fundamentally humanistic principles. But if speech communication teachers are to fill the gap created by the New Philistinism, they must become more vigorous in teaching the principles of human reasoning because their students are not taking sufficient course work in logic. Teachers of speech communication must demand that their students write, rewrite, and write again because these students are not taking advanced courses in English either. Teachers of speech communication must expose their students to the world of political controversy, to the techniques of problem solving through discussion, and to the infinite diversity of human auditors because these students are surely not taking extensive work in political science, philosophy, or anthropology. I am not suggesting that we become Jacks-and-Jills-of-All-Humanistic-Trades. I am merely attempting to point up how loudly the heathens have raged of late and how complicated that has made our jobs as teachers of an essentially humanizing discipline.

During each of the last 10 years, I have taught an undergraduate lecture course in the principles of persuasion. Recently, I have begun to notice how guileless my students seem, how shocked they appear to be when I uncover for them a persuasive ploy or a beguiling piece of sham logic. They seem to blanch, rather visibly, when I suggest that some of their cultural paragons—their mothers, their teachers, their doctors, their newscasters—are persuaders to the core. Oh, yes, they wink knowingly when discussing the persuasive wiles of preachers and presidents and panhandlers, but they are loathe to examine the strategies of the quieter rhetors in their lives.

It is quite possible that my students' inability to understand subtle rhetoric when they see it results from their lack of knowledge of the complex human motivations depicted in that unread Shakespearean play or from their unfamiliarity with such historical personages as Joe McCarthy and Huey Long. Their untutored critical sensibilities, dulled by a pablum of mediated extravaganzas, surely are part of the problem as well. To the extent that our students are ignorant of how they are influenced by their social environment or of how they might effectively marshal their intellectual resources to combat those influences, they will play into the hands of the New Philistines.

Although it is overly grand to suggest that teachers of speech communication are society's last line of defense against the New Philistines, I can think of no great harm it would do for us to think of ourselves in this admittedly exalted way. In the 1980's, speech communication must bend itself to age-old, but increasingly forsaken, tasks. Naturally, it is necessary for us to continue to demonstrate to college administrators that courses in speech communication inculcate practical skills and that our students become more obviously useful people by having had our courses. But the Academy of Ideas also demands something of us. If speech communication is to become the New Humanities, it must listen respectfully to the current din of pragmatism, but it must hearken, too, to the meeker cries of the Old Humanities.

Speech Communication in Applied Settings

Andrew D. Wolvin
Content Consultants: Donna C. Sackett
Prudential Property and Casualty Insurance Company
Jane Work
National Association of Manufacturers

Communication has become a code word in business and industry. Management has come to recognize that many of the management problems facing their organizations are, indeed, problems with communication functions. These communication functions in business and industry are internal and/or external in nature.

THE CHALLENGE OF COMMUNICATION
IN TODAY'S ORGANIZATION

Internal communication functions are those that pertain to the operation of the organization itself. Usually, these functions are perceived as upward, downward, or horizontal in scope. Thus, communication between employees, between supervisor and subordinate, and between supervisors is internal communication. Efforts can be made to establish upward channels of communication whereby employees can communicate more directly with their supervisors—with management and executive officers. And, of course, downward communication—from supervisors to employees—is characteristic of all organizations, particularly in the directive sense of getting the job done.

General Electric has made an effort to improve this communication among employees and supervisors by establishing internal "press conferences"—regularly scheduled forums during which employees can ask questions of General Electric officials. The officials listen and respond to questions about plant procedures and policies. Don Campbell, GE manager of community relations for their Suffolk, Virginia, plant, credits the success of the program to effective communication: "We probably do more listening to employees in this plant than any other plant I know."[1]

While upward and downward communication channels are important formal means of internal communication between supervisors and employees, informal horizontal channels between managers and/or between employees also represent important avenues for the internal communication of an organization. Staff meetings, coffee breaks, luncheons, and even employee recreation associations can serve an organization's internal/informal communication needs. Some organizations even foster the "grapevine" channels as a way of "leaking" important (often unpleasant) information such as impending cutbacks, reductions in force, etc. Communication specialists feel that these informal channels can serve as the key to disseminating information within the organization.

Organizations must deal not only with these internal communication functions but also with external communication needs—communicating with the public. Consequently, organizations have continually expanded budgets for public relations, public affairs, consumer relations, and advertising.[2] It is necessary, of course, for any organization to "sell" its goods, services, programs, and positions on public issues to its constituents. Since the American public is so bombarded with mass communication, the task of capturing attention and getting the message across in advertising has become phenomenal.

COMMUNICATION SKILLS NECESSARY
TO MEET THE CHALLENGE

In order to effectively communicate through internal and external communication channels, individuals must be equipped with extensive job knowledge and substantial communication skills. Several studies of communication in organizations reveal that people need specific skills in order to function effectively in these organizations. They must be able to do good work and to communicate that work in order to achieve success on the job.

At an interesting Speech Communication Association conference on career education held in the summer of 1972, representatives from various career fields (counseling, ministry, law enforcement, sales, management, and education) joined speech communication professors and teachers for a series of forums on the communication competencies necessary for individuals to function effectively in the career world. Considerable emphasis was given to the development of listening and interviewing skills. As a result of their exploration of the implications of these career needs for curriculum development in educational institutions, conference participants suggested that secondary school speech courses develop student competencies in interpersonal communication.[3]

An important survey of people working in business organizations revealed the importance of three human communication activities (in order of respondent ratings): listening; routinely exchanging information; and advising. In this same study, respondents indicated those communication skills that they wished they had studied in college. In order of frequency mentioned, those skills were listening, public speaking, formal writing, small-group communication, "human relations," and persuasion theory.[4]

A recent study appears to reinforce the importance of these communication competencies: When chairpersons of university and college academic departments (other than speech communication departments) were asked what communication skills they perceived as essential to career success in their fields, they stressed the importance of effective listening and clear, concise expression of ideas.[5]

COMMUNICATION TRAINING IN THE ORGANIZATION

In order to effectively meet the challenge of the expanding role of the internal and external communication functions in business/industry/government, many organizations have developed elaborate education and training programs to better prepare their employees to be communicators as well as to perform their specific job skills. The Conference Board conducted a study of major corporations in 1975 and discovered that companies spent about $1.6 billion on in-house education and training activities. Three out of five of the companies surveyed offered courses in supervisory skills as well as in technical/functional skills.[6]

The Conference Board study uses the training program for foremen with General Electric as an example of management development curriculums in industry. The GE foremen's supervisory program includes modules on elements of foremanship; styles of leadership; two-way communication; listening awareness; grievance handling; constructive discipline; facilitating change; interpersonal relationships; job instruction training; labor relations; handling work assignments; improving employee performance; and setting performance standards.[7] It would appear that the entire curriculum deals with communication in specific contexts. Many other corporations offer similar communication training opportunities. Xerox, IBM, AT&T, Western Electric, CBS, Sperry, and General Motors, for instance, have established extensive communication curriculums.

Not only do private corporations provide extensive communication training programs for employees, but also federal agencies offer a variety of education and training opportunities to improve the communication of federal workers. In 1977, 883,087 government workers received 37,464,544 hours of training at a cost of $256,941,055. While much of this training concentrated on specialty and technical subject areas, a sizeable amount of the budget (at an average cost of $7.44 per hour) went for executive and management training during which most of the communication skills are stressed.[8] This author conducts a communication course each year for federal executives who make up the Executive Seminar sponsored by the U.S. Department of State. Increasingly, top-level federal officials must serve as spokespersons for their agencies in dealing with Congress, the public, and other agencies.

IMPLICATIONS FOR THE SECONDARY SCHOOL SPEECH COMMUNICATION CURRICULUM

The need for effective communication skills in business/industry/ government organizations, then, offers a tremendous challenge to educators in today's communication "explosion." And it has caused business and industry officials to turn to teachers as a population for business communicators. This demand for effective communicators is underscored by a report in *Business Week* that indicated teachers are leaving the field of education for the field of business. Employment specialists see the field of education as a source of high-quality personnel because teachers' communication skills have prepared them to motivate, train, and supervise people. Phillip A. Rice, vice-president of human resources at Basic Four Corporation (an Irvine, California, computer manufacturer), emphasized communication skills: "We look upon teachers as a dynamite resource. They're the kind of good communicators we can adapt to our business."[9]

Because business and industry need employees who can communicate, secondary schools ought to provide young people with the necessary communication competencies to function in organizations. Part of their career education should be training in effective speaking and listening so that they can enter the job market with the necessary communication abilities.

It would seem, therefore, that the secondary school curriculum should build on a foundation of communication skills that will enable students to develop the communication abilities necessary to function effectively on the job. In order to assess what this career communication curriculum might include, Michael S. Hanna surveyed personnel officers in Rockford, Illinois. From the responses, Hanna concluded that career communication courses should stress communication skills needed for motivating, delegating authority, listening, giving directions, and solving problems in groups. Less emphasis, he suggested, should be placed on formal presentations and more on leadership and participation in conferences.[10]

Joanne Gurry, a secondary school speech communication teacher in Marshfield, Massachusetts, has described how to implement the objectives of a career education program in the secondary school.[11] Gurry suggests modeling the program on the Sidney Fine hierarchy of human relationships: taking instructions—helping; exchanging information; coaching, persuading, diverting; consulting, instructing, treating; supervising; negotiating; and mentoring. Gurry notes that a curriculum based on the development of such human relationship skills "should reinforce the fundamental concept that communication is inherent to some degree in all careers, that one's ability to communicate . . . is necessary to achieve competence and satisfaction."[12]

In 1977 the Speech Communication Association established a task force to determine guidelines for minimal speaking and listening competencies for high school graduates. Those competencies, based on an extensive review of literature available, provide for specific skills related to occupational communication (e.g., understand directions given by a superior; use appropriate language during employment interviews; distinguish between facts and opinions in labor–management disputes). The complete task force report[13] includes a comprehensive list of those competencies that secondary school students should develop in order to prepare for communicating on the job. The suggested skills closely parallel what the studies of business and industry suggest are important skills for persons in the work force to have.

The tremendous focus today on communication in business/industry/government also has implications for the preparation of students as communication specialists. The old idea that all speech majors could do was teach speech is no longer viable. Given the focus on communication, it is clear that communication specialists are and will continue to be in great demand.

A recent report by the Speech Communication Association Task Force on Alternative Career Opportunities reports on communication positions held by speech communication graduates in a variety of business/industrial/governmental organizations throughout the nation. The respondents' job descriptions reflect the wide range of internal and external communication positions available to communication specialists: editing internal and external publications; designing and producing brochures; managing large meetings; handling public relations; writing speeches and directing internal videotaping; speaking to public groups; working in media relations; managing special events; preparing consumer information; developing community relations; supervising a speakers' bureau; copyediting; directing on-camera activity; writing fund-raising proposals; conducting research through telephone and mail surveys; participating in staff development; supervising student work; preparing information for stockholders; producing slide shows; working as an on-camera reporter; serving as traffic clerk at a TV station; preparing public service announcements; developing brown bag lunch-time seminars for employees; interviewing; diagnosing communication problems.[14] The respondents to this same study were asked to rank, in order of importance, the communication skills that they felt were necessary to function effectively as communication specialists. They identified the following: (1) writing skills; (2) organizing skills; (3) news skills; (4) public speaking skills, analytic skills, and interpersonal skills.[15]

It would appear, then, that the secondary school speech communication curriculum should be at the "core" of career education in order to provide *all* students with the basic communication skills they will need to function effectively on the job and to provide potential speech majors with the foundation skills they will need in colleges and universities as they prepare for careers as communication specialists in business/industry/government organizations. The secondary school speech teacher should not hesitate to send good students into programs that are designed to prepare them for communication careers (not necessarily the traditional, theoretical speech programs but rather programs that offer a theoretical base coupled with such career activities as internships, career counseling, career conferences, and close relationships with the professional community).[16] While the demand for communicators will continue to grow through the 1980's, it is important to recognize that the competition for such positions also will intensify. Because speech communication majors must compete with journalism, English, psychology, and business management majors for the same types of positions, the quality of training is crucial.

THE FUTURE OF COMMUNICATION IN ORGANIZATIONS

The advances of communication in organizations in the 1970's are continuing in the 1980's.[17] As management continues to recognize the importance of effective communication and of the training of employees to be effective communicators, human communication should be central to the functioning of any organization. Organizations may well be forced to deal with the burgeoning information explosion through new, dynamic communication models—approaches that will require communication experts. Paperless offices, for example, based on computers and word processors, may represent the wave of the future. Such advances will mean a radical departure from current work patterns and will require new communication channels and techniques.

Flextime, likewise, may change the nature of communication in organizations as people spend less time together in offices and more time away from the work environment. Again, such a change will require different communication patterns and skills for workers to adapt to less personal contact.

Other influences on the organization in the 1980's may well stem from the need for greater attention to job satisfaction. As the "baby boom" era men and women continue to glut the pyramid of organizations, there will be less room at the "top" for persons who strive for upward mobility. Consequently, it will be necessary to convince people, especially managers, that "up" is not always better and that individual job satisfaction can be achieved in a more stable position. Thus, motivation through job design that breaks down the monotony of doing the same thing for years will be a challenge facing managers.

The changing nature of the work force will also require future adaptation in communication patterns within organizations. As workers continue to age and acquire education (evidenced by the current trends among employees to avoid retirement and to continue their education), management will have to come up with new theories of motivation and productivity. And the communication specialist will be challenged to develop new communication strategies to deal with these changes.

Such changes present an interesting challenge for speech communication educators as they prepare our students to fill the communication needs of the 1980's. Certainly the internal and external functions of all types of organizations will depend on their success.

REFERENCES

1. Kaufman, Steven B. "GE Harmony at Virginia Plant." *The Washington Post,* July 1, 1979. pp. G1, G11.

2. A General Accounting Office report on the "public affairs" (public relations) activities of 31 federal government agencies, for instance, reveals that the agencies spent about $199 million for fiscal year 1975. See: "Difficulties in Evaluating Public Affairs Government-Wide and at the Department of Health, Education, and Welfare." LCD-79-405. Washington, D.C.: U. S. General Accounting Office, 1979. p. 5.

3. Kennicott, Patrick Curtis, and Schuelke, L. David, editors. *Career Communication: Directions for the Seventies.* New York: Speech Communication Association, 1972.

4. Di Salvo, Vincent; Larsen, David C.; and Seiler, William J. "Communication Skills Needed by Persons in Business Organizations." *Communication Education* 25: 269–275; November 1976.

5. Marlier, John T., and Phillips-Madison, Lynda J. "Assessing Needs and Serving Markets." Paper presented at the Speech Communication Association convention, San Antonio, November 1979.

6. Lusterman, Seymour. "Education in Industry." New York: The Conference Board, 1977. p. 2.

7. *Ibid.,* p. 56.

8. "Employee Training in the Federal Service Fiscal Year 1977." Washington, D.C.: U.S. Civil Service Commission Bureau of Training, 1978. pp. 3, 31.

9. "Hard Lessons for Teachers Seeking New Careers." *Business Week* 2609: 116; October 29, 1979.

10. Hanna, Michael S. "Speech Communication Training Needs in the Business Community." *Central States Speech Journal* 29: 171–172; Fall 1978.

11. Gurry, Joanne. "Career Communication in the Secondary School." *Communication Education* 25: 307–316; November 1976.

12. *Ibid.,* p. 311.

13. Bassett, Ronald E.; Whittington, Nilwon; and Staton-Spicer, Ann. "The Basics in Speaking and Listening for High School Graduates: What Should Be Assessed?" *Communication Education* 27: 203–223; November 1978.

14. Blankenship, Jane. "An Inventory of Skills Requirements for a Variety of Non-Teaching Entry Level Jobs in Non-Academic and Academic Settings." Paper presented at the Speech Communication Association convention, San Antonio, November 1979. p. 3.

15. *Ibid.,* p. 5.

16. For a description of such programs, see the following:

McBath, James H., and Burhans, David T., Jr. *Communication Education for Careers.* Urbana, Ill.: ERIC Clearinghouse on Reading and Communication Skills, 1975.

Jamieson, Kathleen M., and Wolvin, Andrew D. "Non-Teaching Careers in Communication: Implications for the Speech Communication Curriculum." *Communication Education* 25: 283–291; November 1976.

17. For an interesting discussion of the future of human communication, see: Jennings, Lane. "The Human Side of Tomorrow's Communications." *The Futurist* 13: 104–109; April 1979. For a discussion of the future of the workplace, see: Kerr, Clark, and Rosow, Jerome M. *Work in America: The Decade Ahead.* New York: Van Nostrand-Reinhold, 1979.

Additional Readings

Kennicott, Patrick C., and Schuelke, L. David, editors. *Career Communication: Directions for the Seventies*. New York: Speech Communication Association, 1972. This report of the proceedings of the 1972 SCA summer conference on career communication identifies communication skills essential for all students to enter the career world in any professional/technical field. While the conference did not deal specifically with preparing the communication specialist, it did highlight the essential role of communication in business, industry, government, and social agencies.

McBath, James H., and Burhans, David T., Jr. *Communication Education for Careers*. Urbana, Ill.: ERIC Clearinghouse on Reading and Communication Skills, 1975. This landmark study surveys the pertinent literature and offers excellent curricular advice for the establishment of programs designed to prepare students for careers as communication specialists in nonacademic settings.

Spicer, Christopher H. "Identifying the Communication Specialist: Implications for Career Education." *Communication Education* 28: 188–198; July 1979. This study reports results of a survey identifying what communication specialists do, as well as what they perceive to be necessary skills to function as communication specialists. The results focus on journalistic and training positions.

CHAPTER 6

Communication Education in the 80's

Kathleen M. Galvin
Pamela J. Cooper
Content Consultants: Kenneth L. Brown
University of Massachusetts
Jo Sprague
San José State University

At the close of 1979, fifth graders in West Warwick, Rhode Island, made their predictions about life in the 1980's. Some of their predictions for the new decade included Christmas trees that will put themselves together; houses that will shrink at the push of a button, making moving a snap; pens that will write automatically as you speak; and video robot machines that will replace teachers and allow students to learn at home.[1] As we read these predictions, we were attracted to the possibility of shrinking schools, allowing us to function as the itinerant rhetorical teachers of ancient Greece, divested of institutionalism, carrying our knowledge from one shady tree to another. As that fantasy faded, we began to speculate on the realistic possibilities for communication education in the 1980's—presented here in terms of the people, the content, the contexts, and the research we envision for the decade.

PEOPLE

Who will be the teachers and/or learners of the 80's? Although our youthful population is shrinking, we will continue to teach speech, theatre, and mass media to children and adolescents, from kindergarten through university. But this young population reflects society's changes. We've all heard the old expression that "kids will be kids," indicating certain developmental constants, but many students we taught in the late 1970's did not look or act very much like many of the students we taught in the late 1960's. And, in the transactional nature of things, we probably do not look or act as we did a decade earlier. In his description of the changing middle class child, psychologist David Elkind describes the current generation as "hurried children" who "grow up too fast, pushed in their early years toward many different kinds of achievement . . . trying to divest themselves of the fear and consequence of failure."[2] In short, these are pressured young people with diffuse goals; they are being pushed to intellectual attainment and self-sufficient maturity by a world of high parental expectations and diverse family styles that force them to grow up quickly. Yet, often the career world is not ready for the starry-eyed graduate. The hurry-up-and-wait generation is upon us: They demand applicable skills rather than a liberal arts approach to learning; yet, they are frustrated in certain attempts to apply those skills in a tight employment situation.

If this is one youthful population, we have to be prepared for another population with nowhere to go and little motivation to push along the way. As the urban–suburban gap worsens and as more city schools face New York–Cleveland–Chicago-type financial crises, the split between the "haves" and "have-nots" will be reflected in more homogeneous schools and in an urban dumping ground of the poor, minorities, and immigrants who believe their future to be limited. These will be the "frustrated children."

The 1970's saw a boom in adult education. Persons from 18 to 80 returned to the classroom in droves for personal development and pleasure—enrolling in such courses as public speaking, improvisational theatre, and media criticism—and for career development—enrolling in such courses as organizational communication, television production, and arts management. This trend shows no sign of declining as increased leisure time, emphasis on self-improvement, and predictable career changes thrust an ever-growing population back into a learning environment. As our elderly population increases, we will need to create communication instruction geared to their needs and capabilities.

Smaller, unique student populations will continue to emerge in the 80's. New waves of refugees will make up the "homeless, tempest-tossed" dreamers attempting to reach the American dream through its educational system. Urban schools will, again, experience an increase of non-English-speaking students in their classrooms. Finally, Public Law 94-142 will continue to mandate regular classroom instruction for handicapped students who will be mainstreamed with greater frequency into the general population.

Juxtaposed to these needs, we predict fewer candidates entering the teaching profession in all areas, including speech communication, due to past difficulties in the job market and expanding alternative opportunities for women in business. This may result in a dearth of young teachers qualified to fill speech and theatre positions in the mid-80's. A recent study by placement directors at Midwestern colleges showed "some demand for teachers of drama and journalism."[3] The drop in the number of qualified teachers, coupled with a predictable decline in the number of communication education graduate students, may well result in a personnel crisis in the 80's. Those who do enter the profession will need specialized training to meet the needs of the unique multi-aged and multicultural populations that will need and expect communication training in the 80's.

CONTENT AND CONTEXTS

We predict some changes in both the content and the education contexts for communication education in the 1980's. The classroom will remain the traditional bastion of speech/theatre education, but there will be a growing emphasis on communication competence. Legislative provisions in Title II of the 1978 Elementary and Secondary Education Act mandate oral competency as part of the basic skills improvement, heralding a demand for teachers and materials geared to the development of oral communicative competence. While such competency training will become the province of all teachers, the drive must be spearheaded by speech communication professionals. Our field will continue to rely on the results of the National Competencies Project, building competence curriculums in the five communication functions of informing, controlling, sharing feelings, ritualizing, and imagining.[4]

The traditional content divisions of public speaking, small groups, interpersonal communication, mass communication, and theatre will be altered as more curriculums are organized around the crucial issues and concerns of contemporary life. Speech communication curriculums will focus on developing at each age level the speech communication competencies needed to function in society. Also, the instructional methods will reflect certain technological and societal changes. We may see computer-assisted public speaking, more communication apprehension labs, and increased creative drama for the elderly.

The strong emphasis on communication training for all teachers that emerged in the 70's is continuing. As Lynn suggests in her review of the literature:

> In brief, today's trainers of teachers appear to be concerned about the need to develop teachers' competencies in areas which, essentially, depend upon knowledge of speech communication: verbal interaction, listening and responding, methods of inquiry, classroom dynamics, interpersonal communication, cross-cultural communication, nonverbal communication, semantics, and the evaluative nature of language.[5]

The 80's will see even greater stress on communication as the essence of teaching.

Those who accept a systems orientation will continue to stress the importance of communication education within significant interpersonal contexts such as the family or the business organization. Such an approach assumes that success in changing an individual's communication behavior depends on altering the systems in which he or she functions. Thus, if the familial system negates most of the communication behaviors taught in school, it is unlikely that a student will receive reinforcement for trying new behaviors; conversely, if certain desirable communication behaviors are supported within the family system, the student's behavior should reflect this.[6] In concrete terms, a 14-year-old's communication behavior may be directly affected by his or her parents' communication behavior rather than by a course that teaches behaviors contradictory to everyday life experience. Altering the behavior of a personnel manager in a school context may not have much effect on his or her job performance if the other members of the personnel system maintain their rigid behavior code.

Thus, communication educators are more likely to take their expertise to the system, teaching communication skills to married couples or to whole families through religious or private instruction in hopes of affecting behavior change in contexts other than a school setting. They will also continue to provide on-site instruction in organizational communication in an attempt to alter interpersonal systems in the workplace. Concurrent with this, students will be given more "real world" experiences. By encouraging students to utilize their skills in the form of internships, community service projects, and observations of communication in various contexts, communication educators will link the classroom to the world at large.

RESEARCH

In conjunction with the changes in the people, content, and contexts of communication education, the research in the 80's will reflect the research of the 70's, but with unique dimensions. In order to meet the challenges of developing the curriculums and of teaching within varying contexts, communication education research in the 1980's must address two major questions: (1) What do we need to know in order to make speech curriculums more applicable to the students of the 80's? (2) What do we need to know concerning communication in the classroom to help *all* teachers?

The major thrust for communication research as it relates to speech curriculum development involves the determining of communication competencies. The Speech Communication Association's National Project on Speech Communication Competencies provides an excellent starting place for such research.[7] Additional experimental and field research needs to be conducted both to determine whether students can cognitively and affectively meet the competencies outlined by the Project and to detect ways in which the curriculums can be changed to reflect those competencies. Boileau, for example, argues that most curriculum guides in speech communication ignore the stages of cognitive development.[8] The same might also be said concerning affective development. More research such as that reported by Ritter, Delia, and others[9] needs to be conducted and the findings used to create curriculums based on the communication competencies to be attained at various age levels. Such research can, in turn, suggest activities that speech/theatre teachers can utilize effectively to develop these competencies.

The impact of communication education research will extend far beyond our own classrooms. With the increased awareness by educators of the central role that communication plays in the teaching/learning process, the decade of the 80's marks a time in which considerable opportunity exists for speech educators to make significant contributions to the education of all teachers. What must we do to influence teacher education? While several ideas come to mind, three overriding concerns should guide all communication education research.

First, communication education research should focus on communication variables such as language, perception, and feedback. For example, we know little concerning the nature, use, and influence of feedback (as a regulator, reinforcer, and clarifier) in the classroom. In much educational research, communication has been only indirectly examined.

Second, communication theory should be utilized in classroom research. Most educational research has utilized psychological theories, such as the stimulus–response and cognitive field theories, to explain learning and instruction. Naturally these theories should not be ignored. However, communication theories of meaning, perception, interpersonal relationships, language, etc., should be combined with psychological theories if we are to build communication-based theories of learning and instruction.

Third, communication education research should be done within classroom contexts. Too often we have applied research findings from other contexts to the classroom. For example, researchers have found that concrete messages facilitate more information recall and more accurate perceptions than do vague, ambiguous, abstract messages.[10] However, this research was conducted outside the instructional context. Will these findings hold true in an environment in which the mediating variables of grades, relationships with the instructor, and subject matter differences come into play? Research conducted in other contexts should not serve as the primary basis for suggesting classroom practices for preservice and in-service teachers.

Within the context of these general guidelines, several variables need to be examined: teacher variables (demographic, training, and personality); student variables (demographic and personality); teaching/learning process variables (teacher classroom behavior, student classroom behavior, student–teacher interaction); and product variables (short-term and long-term changes in students as a result of classroom interaction).

In terms of the teacher, several communication-related variables have yet to be examined. For example, what effect does teacher self-concept have on the teaching methods chosen? Does a teacher's self-concept relate to teacher bias or teacher expectancies? What effect does self-concept have on teacher's communication style? Although we are beginning to understand how teacher expectancies and biases are communicated to students, we still know little about the origin of these two phenomena. An examination of teacher variables such as teacher self-concept, communication apprehension, receiver apprehension, and communicator style may "shed light" on these phenomena. Although demographic variables such as age, sex, and race have been examined as they relate to job performance in nonacademic settings, they have not often been studied as they relate to teachers and teaching. Examining these variables may tell us much concerning effective teachers.

Communication researchers have examined several major student variables—for example, oral communication apprehension, receiver apprehension, writing apprehension, language development, and social perspective taking. Once again we are fairly sure these variables affect student learning. However, we are unclear as to their origin or how to effectively and efficiently treat them. In addition, other student variables need examination. For example, what effect do student expectations have on communication in the classroom? How are these expectations communicated to the teacher? What variables affect a student's preference for multimedia vs. linear modes of instruction? By what teaching methods do field-dependent students learn best? By what teaching methods do field-independent students learn best? How is communication affected by those two variables?

Teaching/learning process variables are at the very heart of teaching and are, perhaps, where our communication education researchers' efforts should be focused. Patterns of pupil/teacher interaction, methods of describing classroom talk, teacher questioning/response behavior, and pupil questioning/response behavior are only a few of the processes that need clarification. Also important to investigate are the uses of language in instruction and the influence of these uses on student cognitive and affective learning. For example, research should be aimed at understanding better the language of instruction (Do teachers use language in ways that are unique to teaching?), the language of subject matter (To what extent is achievement in subject matter areas dependent on mastery of the language of subject matters?), and language uses and cognition (How do teachers use language to focus attention on a learning task, to encourage students to search for and evaluate information, etc.?).

From a communication perspective, a variety of process variables should be examined simultaneously. Multivariate research designs enable us to examine relationships among process variables—to determine what affects the process of the classroom and, in turn, what effects are produced by these processes.

The major product variable examined in most educational research has been student achievement. Perhaps it is time to examine other, equally important product variables such as improved self-concept, improved teacher/student relationships, and more positive attitudes toward learning and the subject matter.

The ultimate goal of communication education researchers should be to design research in which teacher, student, process, and/or product variables are combined, thus increasing the likelihood that the results will be of use to educators. From a communication perspective, research that does not combine variables in this manner does not tell us a great deal. For example, to know that teachers talk more than students is not particularly helpful unless we know why and/or what effect this phenomenon has on students.

If we follow the directions outlined, several important results should be accomplished. We should know more about what communication competencies teachers really need in order to produce student change and growth. We should have a better understanding of what teaching methods are most useful with various students and under varying conditions. Information such as this should, in turn, lead us to a better idea of how to evaluate teaching. Ultimately, this information should enable us to begin to structure communication-based theories of instruction and learning.

One might be overwhelmed, and even discouraged, by what needs to be accomplished by communication education researchers. Research on teaching, particularly when conducted from a communication perspective, can produce practical, empirically based information for the improvement of classroom teaching. Indeed, we've already begun to produce such information. What we must understand is that the production of this information will take considerable time and effort. Certainly it won't all be accomplished in the 1980's or by communication educators alone. Interdisciplinary approaches are not only desirable but also necessary if we are to make headway toward formulating concrete suggestions concerning the teaching/learning process.

As our field enters a new era, its success or failure rests on our shoulders. In his description of *The Future of Man,* Pierre Teilhard De Chardin writes: "The whole future of the Earth, as of religion, seems to me to depend on the awakening of our faith in the future."[11] Just as the 10-year-olds in Rhode Island predicted a better future in the 80's, so, too, we need to display a faith in this decade of communication education.

REFERENCES

1. *Chicago Tribune,* January 18, 1980.

2. Elkind, David. "Growing Up Faster." *Psychology Today* 12: 38–47; September 1979.

3. Carmichael, Carole. "Teachers Needed in Many Subjects Despite Cutbacks." *Chicago Tribune,* February 17, 1980.

4. Allen, R.R., and Brown, Kenneth L., editors. *Developing Communication Competence in Children.* Skokie, Ill.: National Textbook Co., 1976.

5. Lynn, Elizabeth M. *Improving Classroom Communication: Speech Communication Instruction for Teachers.* Falls Church, Va.: Speech Communication Association, 1976.

6. Galvin, Kathleen. "A Critical Analysis of Communication Instruction in Current Marital Interaction Programs." Paper presented at the Speech Communication Association convention, 1978.

7. Allen, R.R., and Brown, Kenneth L., editors. *op. cit.*

8. Boileau, Donald. "An Investigation of the Effects of Persuasive Speech: Application of Piaget's Developmental Theory." *Speech Teacher,* January 1975. pp. 13–14.

9. Ritter, Ellen. "Social Perspective Taking Ability, Cognitive Complexity and Listener Adapted Communication in Early and Late Adolescence." *Communication Monographs* 46: 40–52; 1979.
See also articles by Delia and others appearing in *Communication Monographs* 46: 231–282; 1979.

10. Goss, B. "The Effect of Sentence Context on Associations to Ambiguous, Vague, and Clear Norms." *Speech Monographs* 39: 286–289; 1972.

11. Teilhard De Chardin, Pierre. *The Future of Man.* New York: Harper & Row, 1969.

Additional Readings

Allen, R. R., and Brown, Kenneth L., editors. *Developing Communication Competence in Children.* Skokie, Ill.: National Textbook Co., 1976. Published as the result of a major study of communication competence in children, this text contains a review of each of the three strands of the study—the literature review, the field study, and the questionnaire component—culminating in the results of the final synthesis conference. The well-developed literature section has value for anyone interested in how children learn language codes, roles, and norms, as well as the affective components and application of communication. The synthesis chapter provides a categorization of the development of communication competence and communication acts that is useful to teachers and researchers.

Dunkin, Michael, and Biddle, Bruce. *The Study of Teaching.* New York: Holt, Rinehart and Winston, 1974. The authors of this text summarize knowledge concerning teaching that has been developed through research. The book is organized into three parts. The first part presents a model for classroom teaching, methodological matters students need to understand in order to deal with research on teaching, and notions that have grown up in education concerning teaching and its improvement. The second portion of the text reviews studies and presents findings on classroom climate, classroom management, the classroom as a social system, knowledge and intellect, logic and linguistics, and sequential patterns of classroom behavior. The final section of the text provides tabular summaries of the research presented in the second part and sets forth recommendations for future research.

Halliday, Mina G., editor. *A Guide for Teaching Speech Today: Six Alternative Approaches.* Skokie, Ill.: National Textbook Co., 1979. Prepared by secondary school speech educators, the text presents a rationale, behavioral objectives, a content/activities outline, and evaluation procedures for each of the six approaches—career communication, interpersonal communication, survey approach, group dynamics approach, public speaking approach, and receiver-based communication. The materials in the text are extremely practical and provide an understanding of what a well-developed course in speech communication should do for the student.

Lynn, Elizabeth. *Improving Classroom Communication: Speech Communication Instruction for Teachers.* Falls Church, Va.: Speech Communication Association, 1976. Based on Lynn's dissertation, this text provides the following: (1) a rationale for the development of courses in classroom communication, (2) a survey of the current status of courses and programs in classroom communication, and (3) a list of resources appropriate to the area. Lynn demonstrates the interrelationship between research in speech communication and education as it applies to classroom interaction. The text provides valuable practical information for anyone contemplating designing and teaching a classroom communication course.

CHAPTER 7

Communication Theory

B. Aubrey Fisher
Content Consultants: Edward M. Bodaken
University of Southern California
C. David Mortensen
University of Wisconsin—Madison

One of the curiosities of human behavior is the tendency to designate certain points in time as demarcations between past and future. Rites of passage which come readily to mind include one's 16th birthday (driver's license), one's 18th birthday (voting), one's 40th birthday (lamentation of lost youth), and any year divisible by 10 (a new decade). As we reach such milestones, we invariably set aside some time for taking stock of the past and predicting trends for the future. Because such a function seems presumptuous, at best, I shall attempt to avoid pontificating and recommending in favor of observing and speculating.

Because the dates of a decade possess only arbitrary significance, some point of reference would be helpful in order to assess the present status of communication theory in pedagogy. An obvious point of reference conveniently presents itself—1970. In that year of transition, the Speech Communication Association (SCA) sponsored a summer conference with the theme, "Implications of Recent Research for Speech Communication Education," for teachers in elementary, secondary, and higher education. The proceedings[1] of that conference provide not only some description of communication theory in 1970 but also some basis for speculating about the function of communication theory in communication education during the 1980's.

COMMUNICATION THEORY—1970's

The first observation about communication theory in 1970 is that there was an explicit need for a comprehensive theory of communication. With such a theory, many felt they would know what to teach as well as how to teach these applications of communication theory in the classroom.

A second observation is that there was a lingering feud between proponents of two different approaches to communication: the philosophical/humanistic approach and the behavioral/scientific approach. Some rhetoricians characterized behavioral science as "an ideology characterized primarily by its mindless . . . vacuity"[2]; some behavioral scientists referred to rhetoric as "blind reliance on the past" and "attempts to turn us backward."[3] Such polemics stemmed principally from a difference in the techniques used to observe and research communicative phenomena—criticism vs. statistics, the qualitative vs. the quantitative.

Third, the predominant criterion used to judge educational or curricular excellence in 1970 was *relevance*. That year reflected the stinging aftermath of Kent State, the student revolts of the late 1960's, and the anti-war campus protests. As a result, educators sought to institute new courses (e.g., black rhetoric, urban crises, political persuasion) and to make existing courses more relevant to contemporary 1970. All education, including communication, felt the impact of this demand for relevance, a reflection of then contemporary society. The extraordinary became the ordinary.

A fourth element of communication theory of 1970 was the shift from a message-centered (or source-centered) version of communication to a receiver-centered approach. The receiver, not the source or the message, was considered to be the dominant force in controlling the effect of communication. The emphasis in many classrooms shifted from constructing a message on the basis of some optimal model or "ideal" to analyzing the audience and then constructing appeals appropriate to the receivers. Communicators were taught to plan strategies; effectiveness was a measure of success in securing the desired audience response.

Finally, communication theory emphasized its manipulative function almost to the exclusion of other functions. Persuasion was virtually synonymous with communication. The shift from a message to a receiver orientation did not change the basic function of communication —"affecting changes in audience behaviors"[4]; it changed only the methods of bringing about such effects. Because of this unifunctional view of communication, the theory focused on persuasion, which led to indiscriminate borrowing from the behavioral sciences (principally social psychology) in order to provide theoretical assumptions about communication. Many of the terms/variables popular at the time (e.g., source credibility, ego-involvement, fear appeals) were borrowed directly from theories of attitude change within social psychology and used freely as theoretical concepts inherent in communication.

COMMUNICATION THEORY—1980's

The 1970's witnessed numerous changes in communication theory and inquiry. While the field is no closer to a single, comprehensive communication theory, our attitude has changed markedly. As communication students/teachers/scholars we continue to use different theories, but we seem satisfied with the presence of differing, and even competing, theoretical perspectives.[5] Today the emphasis in communication theory is less on what *should* be done and more on what *is* being done by teachers/scholars in communication. The result is an increased tolerance of, and even an appreciation for, diverse approaches to theory, inquiry, and teaching.

The 1970 cry for relevance became the back-to-basics movement of 1980.[6] Nearly everyone seems distressed by the deplorable quality of reading, writing, mathematics, and speaking skills in the present generation of students. The neorelevant courses created in the 1970's are now all but extinct, and the emphasis is on teaching the fundamental skills of the "3 R's" and beyond.

The division between rhetoric and behavioral science, evidenced in the 1970 conference, was probably symptomatic of the death theories of the feud between historical/critical and empirical scholarship. Even though a few disgruntled isolationists remain, they are fewer in number. A spirit of cooperation prevails, for the most part, and often reflects a mutual and educated appreciation for one another's views. Communication theory today encompasses a diversity of methods, functions, and settings.

A receiver-centered orientation to communication has, generally speaking, gone the way of a source/message-centered orientation. The trend now is toward a more global view of the entire communicative process. Rather than conceptualizing communication as a process in which the receiver controls the source (or vice versa), most contemporary theorists view the communicative process holistically. The orientation, thus, resides within the process in which the various components are related to one another interdependently. The former view sought to understand the communicative process from the perspective of a principal component; the contemporary view seeks to understand all components as they are interrelated within the global process.

That process orientation has led to a different view of how humans function within communication. No longer is communication thought to perform primarily a manipulative function; rather, communication functions to create and maintain some relationship among the interactants. A persuader–persuadee relationship is only one communicative relationship and certainly neither the most important nor the most typical. Communication can involve friendly, egalitarian, reciprocal, complementary, authoritative, marital, familial, and a host of other human relationships.

The preceding discussion does not attempt any comprehensive, state-of-the-art analysis of communication theory. Nor does it include any specific discussion of theory per se. It is intended to illustrate some shifts in assumptions that may be said to characterize contemporary thinking about communication in the broadest possible sense (that is, communication theory). Such assumptions eventually find their way into the curriculums and the pedagogical techniques employed by teachers at every level of education.

IMPLICATIONS FOR EDUCATION

I echo the sentiment expressed by Gerry Miller at the 1970 SCA conference: ". . . my remarks constitute a plea for continued evolution, rather than a call for revolution in speech communication education."[7] I have always distrusted those who claim to have the solution to educational problems. Such solutions invariably advocate sweeping changes and promise an educational panacea. Nearly all involve pie-in-the-sky philosophizing and considerable arrogance. I feel uneasy enough in my present role of seer and, therefore, will identify only a few general trends that seem to be evolving in the field of speech communication education.

The first, and perhaps most notable, evolutionary trend in communication education concerns the first (or "basic") course. I have taught that first course in several high schools and directed it at the university level. My impression is that at either level the first course is the same conceptually and pedagogically. In 1970 the primary emphasis of the first course was public speaking.[8] Although most first courses probably retain this emphasis, a cursory examination of currently available textbooks and college curriculums reveals a clear trend toward greater variety in the basic or entering-level courses. Public speaking is not being discarded; rather, other functions and settings of human communication, in addition to public speaking, are also considered basic or fundamental to a student's training in communicative skills.

The time of *a* first course in communication education may be past. At least two curricular alternatives seem to be gaining popularity. One approach is to provide several different first courses that may emphasize different settings, different functions, or different modes of human communication. That is, first courses might be offered in public speaking, group decision making, and/or interpersonal communication.

A second curricular alternative is to provide a single course that includes such variety within its parameters. But such a first course would not treat topics of several first courses as independent units (i.e., a unit on public speaking, a unit on group discussion, etc.) in a simple potpourri. Rather, units in such a course would involve communicative functions common to a variety of settings. For example, social control could be a course unit that would be applicable to several different exercises and settings of social control: delivering a persuasive speech, establishing a complementary relationship during conversation, dealing with deviant members during group interaction, or analyzing commercial advertising in the mass media. Such a course would emphasize the functions served by communication, along with the different concomitant skills necessary to deal with those functions in various communicative settings. Such a course, appropriately titled "fundamentals" or "principles" of speech communication, retains public speaking but treats it (and other settings) as a context in which to perform some communicative function rather than an end in itself. In this way, the emphasis in the first course shifts from teaching skills for skills' sake to teaching functional skills so that students can communicate more effectively in all settings.

Speech communication has long suffered from an identity problem both within and without the field.[9] Nevertheless, one of the oddities in education is the need to defend the credibility, and often the fundamental necessity, of speech communication training during the present back-to-basics push in public education. Of course, the identity crisis involves a complex set of issues, but the current evolutionary trend toward defining communication as relationships should go a long way toward alleviating the image of speech communication as a "frill" course. The SCA has recently sponsored a series of public service television spot announcements characterizing communicating as the "fourth R"—*relating*. This nationwide campaign identifies training in speech communication consistent with the current trend in communication theory. Communication—relating to other human beings—is a basic

64

skill. Coupled with the viewing of communication as the basic skill of relating to others is the reconceptualizing of communication as a functional process. Each individual communicator contributes to the process but does not define or control it. Communication is *all* of the process. Communicators, acting together, create the relationship. And in most communicative situations, speech is the principal vehicle for relating/communicating. Communicative effectiveness is a characteristic of the whole relationship, the entire interaction, and not merely what one communicator does when contributing to the relationship.

Pedagogically the view of communication as the process of creating/maintaining relationships creates new concepts for teaching speech communication. The emphasis shifts from what *should* be done (e.g., no more "model" speeches) to what *is* done during communication—from the ideal to the practical, from the prescriptive to the descriptive. Communicating effectively requires that the communicator be sensitive to the developing relationship and contribute appropriate actions. Pedagogical emphasis shifts, therefore, from techniques that teach the "correct" or the "best" way to communicate to those that teach the basic (differentiated from "technical") skill of assessing communicative relationships and communicating appropriately within that relationship.

Traditionally speech communication has emphasized rationality. We have taught rules of evidence, forms of support, organizational patterns, soundness of argument, etc., as structures or skills fundamental to all "good" or "effective" communication. In doing so, we have often pointed to Aristotle as the basis for our reliance on the criterion of rationality. But we have probably misinterpreted the still timely advice of Aristotle (and other classical theorists) whose rhetorical theory was situationally based. Rationality was extremely important in deliberative situations (with the goal of decision making or problem solving), and our traditional pedagogy concerned itself almost exclusively with such situations. But most communicative situations, such as day-to-day interactions during a normal human existence, are epideictic, and the criterion of rationality is simply inappropriate. Viewing communication as a process of relating, thus, returns communication/rhetoric to a situation-specific theoretical basis. Criteria change from one situation to another; a single criterion (such as rationality) is impractical.

A POSTSCRIPT

Communication theory in the 1980's incorporates a diversity of perspectives and methods aimed at describing and explaining how humans actually establish relationships with one another. Pedagogical practices, however, have not kept pace with advances in the theoretical/research emphasis on the global view of communication as a functional process. Communicating remains a basic skill—relating to others. The implications for communication education focus on continuing the evolutionary trend in revising the nature of the basic course(s) in communication.

If the past teaches us any lesson at all, we should be well aware that too much disparity exists between our basic courses that we teach as fundamental skills and our theory/research that we conduct in discussions limited to ourselves. Perhaps that disparity is one reason why we claim to be misunderstood by educators outside our field and why we often find ourselves defending our significance in the curriculum, particularly at the high school/college undergraduate level. An integration of theory and pedagogy may be a first step toward recognized respectability squarely within the back-to-basics movement, the hallmark of American education in the 1980's.

REFERENCES

1. Sillars, Malcolm O., editor. "Proceedings, Speech Communication Association Summer Conference VI. Theme: Implications of Recent Research for Speech Communication Education." New York: the Association, 1970. (Mimeo.)

2. *Ibid.,* p. 50.

3. *Ibid.,* pp. 109, 110.

4. *Ibid.,* p. 40.

5. Fisher, B. Aubrey. *Perspectives on Human Communication.* New York: Macmillan, 1978.

6. Ritter, Ellen M. " 'Back to Basics' and Accountability Issues in Secondary School Speech Education." *Communication Education* 27: 111–126; 1978.

7. Sillars, Malcolm O., editor. *op cit.,* p. 39.

8. See: Gibson, James W., and others. "The First Course in Speech: A Survey of U.S. Colleges and Universities." *Speech Teacher* 19: 13–20; 1970.
Friar, Don. "Methods and Trends in the Junior College Speech Course." *Western Speech* 34: 148–153; 1970.
Gibson, James W., and others. "The Basic Course in Speech at U.S. Colleges and Universities: III." *Communication Education* 29: 1–9; 1980.

9. McBath, James H., and Jeffrey, Robert C. "Defining Speech Communication." *Communication Education* 27: 181–188; 1978.

Additional Readings

Arnold, Carroll, and Bowers, John Waite, editors. *Handbook of Rhetorical and Communication Theory.* Boston: Allyn and Bacon, In press. This collection of state-of-the-art essays within a single volume is intended to cover the "waterfront" of contemporary thought among communication scholars. Intended as a comprehensive reference work, this handbook unites the essays under the common umbrella of functions performed by human communication.

Fisher, B. Aubrey. *Perspectives on Human Communication.* New York: Macmillan, 1978. Four perspectives of human communication are presented as alternative conceptualizations of the communication process currently practiced by communication theorists/researchers/teachers. The book details each of the perspectives and illustrates how the perspective used to view communication determines the significance, definition, and even existence of key concepts (e.g., meaning, feedback, message, process) associated with communication.

Knapp, Mark. *Social Intercourse: From Greeting to Goodbye.* Boston: Allyn and Bacon, 1978. Knapp's college textbook emphasizes the processes of developing, maintaining, and terminating social relationships. The view of communication is virtually synonymous with human relationships.

Miller, Gerald R., editor. *Explorations in Interpersonal Communication.* Beverly Hills, Calif.: Sage, 1976. This collection of essays provides a cross-section of contemporary and traditional thought about conceptualizing communication. The readings range from reports of sophisticated research studies to general thinkpieces.

Watzlawick, Paul; Beavin, Janet H.; and Jackson, Don D. *Pragmatics of Human Communication.* New York: Norton, 1967. This volume by three psychotherapists is the classic statement of the "interactional view" of communication, a systems look at human communication inaugurated and developed by the colleagues and protegés of Gregory Bateson.

CHAPTER 8

Intercultural Communication
Molefi Kete Asante

Content Consultants: Tulsi B. Saral
Governors State University
Erika Vora
St. Cloud State University

Intercultural communication is both a theoretical and a practical field. The word *communication* is derived from the Latin *communis,* meaning *common,* from which we get such terms as *community* and *communion.* At the theoretical level, intercultural communication scholars are concerned with explaining how messages are transmitted effectively and with fostering understanding among individuals from different cultures. These scholars test their theories through observation, experimentation, and content analysis. At the practical level, intercultural communicators interact across cultural frontiers in an effort to establish common ground. As a growing area of emphasis, intercultural communication has come to command more and more attention from both theorists and practitioners.

There are two major trends in the study and teaching of intercultural communication: *cultural criticism* and *cultural dialogue.* The cultural critic views the intercultural communication situation from the position of an observer interested in *discovering, isolating,* and *eliminating* communication barriers between people of different cultural backgrounds. Given an intercultural situation, the cultural critic is able to discover the underlying obstacles to the communication and, once those obstacles are isolated, to propose a solution. Thus, in the case of a Brazilian–American business interaction that seems to have been derailed over the missed cultural cues from both sides, the cultural critic would be determined to discover the causes of the missed cues, isolate those causes, and propose changes. If the missed cue were that the American insisted on meeting at a given time, while the Brazilian seemed to be indicating more social contact prior to the business meeting, then that cue would have be isolated from all of the other communications that may have occurred in the meeting between the communicators. The future will see the cultural critics of all societies adjust to the rapid growth in genres of communication for business, theatre, law, and politics. Even here, however, the cultural critic will be called upon to make some sense out of the situations that occur between intercultural communicators. In effect, the cultural critic operates on the assumption that the cultural problems that impinge upon interactions can be eliminated by making the communicators aware of each other's cultural cues. Much of the work emanating from the psychological and anthropological fields is cultural criticism.

Cultural dialogue, on the other hand, is devoted to the process of communicating, the interacting among and engaging with cultures. The cultural dialogist seeks to better the condition of human beings in the world by examining the various ways in which human communication is constrained by culture, with the intent of perfecting the transmission of messages with understanding. Hence, the scholars who call themselves cultural dialogists are primarily and fundamentally involved in the betterment of the intercultural communication practice. Many persons involved in intercultural communication, such as international consultants to multinational corporations, counselors to foreign students, diplomats, international business executives, and members of such groups as the Peace Corps and ACTION, consider the work of the cultural dialogist significant to their success. They need to know how to demystify the intercultural communication experience, how to communicate with a person who has a totally different world orientation, and how best to prepare for intercultural encounters. The cultural dialogist studies cultures with the aim of demonstrating communication in effective use.

Intercultural communication effectiveness can be taught in two principal ways: *cultural specific* and *cultural general.* When a group or a single person is preparing, say, to visit another culture, the intercultural communication preparation may be cultural specific. Information is normally provided about the history, language, life-styles, politics, and religions of the specific people; information on the climate and geography may also be included. Such information is geared to helping the communicator cope with unexpected issues, problems, or communication expressions. The effectiveness of the preparation may depend upon how well the specific information is presented and understood. If the group is preparing to travel to the Akan area of Ghana, West Africa, the cultural specific approach would be to provide the members of the group with an overview of the West African region of the world, the place of Ghana in that region, and the culture of the Akan within Ghana, and with some specific information about the cultural values of the Akan people—i.e., use of the left hand is prohibited, shoes must be removed before the Asantehene, etc. The cultural specific approach was used very effectively in the United States during the early years of the Peace Corps. In recent years, intercultural communication trainers have spent more time on cultural general programs to prepare those anticipating a sojourn in a foreign culture. The cultural general program is designed to give prospective intercultural communicators an overview of values, cultures, verbal and nonverbal behaviors, and attitudes without specific reference to any particular culture. Thus, the group planning to travel to Ghana would be trained how to interact with any person from any culture with whom they wanted to communicate. The users of both approaches to training find their resources in the work of researchers who have spent many years observing intercultural communication behaviors.

The teaching of intercultural communication has become one of the most challenging areas of pedagogy. Because of the increase in international travel and activity, the student of intercultural communication finds a ready source of examples, illustrations, and experiences. Teaching intercultural communication requires knowledge and sensitivity. It is normally considered important that intercultural communication teachers possess a wide knowledge of the subject and an openness to other cultures, if they are to provide effective instruction in intercultural communication. The experience of many teachers indicates that it is also an effective pedagogical practice to have a multicultural class, if possible. In this way, students are able to practice some of the theories they read about. Furthermore, students from different cultures provide the teacher with an excellent source for examples. Students may then be asked to comment on the values, social status structures, behavioral patterns, customs, attitudes, and language issues of various cultures.

Research in intercultural communication will profitably turn toward more value and power analyses. Rather than how non-Americans fit into the American value system, this new research will relate values from culture to culture. Power relations have seldom been analyzed by intercultural communication scholars. Future researchers will, of necessity, have to deal with some of the more intractable issues facing the international community. For example, new research on the Arab–Israeli, Japanese–Korean, Ibo–Hausa, and Cuban–Puerto Rican cultural rights must be conducted. It is to be expected that the work of future researchers in intercultural communication will contribute to the solution of world problems.

Actually, the shift in the world's money resources will greatly affect our intercultural interactions. Patterns established over the last 500 years are beginning to be broken, and non-Western nations are asserting their newly found power. Such shifts in the power relations of nations certainly will affect how the Spaniard views the Nigerian, for example, or how the Norwegian views the Saudi Arabian. These examples will be multiplied thousands of times because the operative difference in human relationships will be new perceptions of the communicators. However, the average communicator in the 1980's is not likely to be cognizant of the changes in any mystical sense; these changes will simply occur as the world becomes a more equitable place in which to live.

There seems to be an inexorable drive toward political freedom for peoples who have been subjugated and denied national expression. I predict that the areas of research cited above will become the most discussed intercultural areas in the next few years. Ethnic populations who live in societies dominated by larger ethnic groups will seek either a greater share in the governing process or complete political autonomy. The intercultural communicationist, therefore, must be capable of and willing to explore the possibilities of communication in any power situation. Consider the debate between Arabs and Israelis in the Middle East. It is a debate that will center on political, historical, and social realities. But since all debates are symbolic and represent communication attempts, the intercultural communicationist of the future will want to monitor this situation for communicative effectiveness even at the personal level of interactants. Recognizing the cultural backgrounds of the communicators, as well as their historical realities, will be absolutely essential.

Furthermore, the intercultural communicationist will have to become accustomed to the world outside his or her own culture. Foreign languages, recently debased in American education, are finding their way back into the educational process. This development is not only significant but also necessary for intercultural communicators. To illustrate the need for increased awareness of other cultures, it was reported recently that only 5 of the 27 Americans stationed in the American embassy of an East African country could speak Kiswahili, the language of the people.

Finally, since most of the nations of the world are caught in an international communication system that neither is designed for them nor seeks to serve them, a redress in the international communication order should occur in the 1980's. Indeed, it is inevitable that as resources change hands, many of the old ways we have known will disappear. And with the disappearance of the inequities in the economic, political, and communication spheres, there should be greater harmony among peoples of the world. As intercultural communication scholars seek to explain how we can transmit messages with fidelity to those of different cultures, they are striving for the perfect moment of intercultural innocence when communicators experience true harmony.

Additional Readings

Asante, Molefi; Newmark, E.; and Blake, C., editors. *The Handbook of Intercultural Communication:* Beverly Hills, Calif.: Sage, 1979. A comprehensive study of the communication process in its national and international dimensions.

Casmir, F., editor. *International and Intercultural Communication.* Washington, D.C.: Academic Press, 1979. A collection of articles on intercultural communication by numerous writers in the intercultural area.

Hoopes, David. *Overview of Intercultural Education, Training and Research.* Washington, D.C.: BCIU/Sietar, 1979. An essential overview of the practical bases of intercultural theory.

Newmark, E., and Asante, Molefi. *Intercultural Communication: Theory Into Practice.* Falls Church, Va.: SCA/ERIC, 1976. An introductory guide for cultural trainers and teachers.

Prosser, Michael. *Cultural Dialogue.* Dubuque, Iowa: Brown Co., 1978. A review of the theoretical development of intercultural communication.

Smith, Arthur. *Transracial Communication.* Englewood Cliffs, N.J.: Prentice-Hall, 1973. The first book to deal with interracial communication from a theoretical perspective.

CHAPTER 9

Directions for
Interpersonal Communication Research

Mary Anne Fitzpatrick
Content Consultants: Joseph N. Cappella
University of Wisconsin—Madison
Malcolm R. Parks
University of Washington

The predictions in this chapter about directions for the field of interpersonal communication in the 80's result from two predominant trends in theory and research in the latter part of the 70's. The first is the movement away from the traditional study of persuasion and attitude change. For many years, the study of interpersonal communication was almost synonymous with the study of effects of certain combinations of message, source, and receiver variables on the attitudes and beliefs of respondents. Interpersonal communication scholars were concerned solely with how certain source and message characteristics might combine to affect a receiver.[1] Although some interest in studying this process remains, it no longer forms the core area of interpersonal study. When the persuasive process is considered, it is examined in terms of how individuals in particular relationships go about "getting their own way."[2]

The second trend emerged as the field moved away from this almost exclusive concern with persuasion. During this time we began some intellectual soul-searching about the appropriate way to study interpersonal phenomena. Scholars proposed a number of different approaches to the construction of interpersonal communication theories.

Basically concerned with issues in the philosophy of science, these approaches were hotly debated; yet little substantive information about interpersonal communication was generated. There were no massive paradigm shifts, and as Donn Byrne once observed about the nature of such debates, "when all is said and done, everyone goes back to their own sandboxes."[3]

Back in their own sandboxes, slightly enlightened, yet not totally reformed by these Savonarolas, scholars in interpersonal communication need to revitalize the business of communication research. One possible direction for our work in the 80's is to reconsider some of the basic questions in communication: How are messages produced? How are they interpreted? What effect do they have?[4]

In the 60's and the 70's, research and theory in interpersonal communication focused on the production and effects of messages. The focus for the 80's will be the question of how messages are interpreted. The central concern for interpersonal scholars of the 80's will not be what they say or what effect it has, but rather, what they mean by what they say. More broadly, the fundamental issue will be a consideration of the question of meaning.

The question of meaning is addressed by all communication scholars, not only those who study interpersonal communication. However, the interpersonal scholar labors under an extra burden because how communicators assign meaning to messages is intricately tied to the relationship that has evolved between them. Consequently, to examine the communication that takes place between people, the interpersonal scholar must first define the relationship between those individuals.

Explanations of communication in relationships will address the issue of meaning under two substantially different theoretical frameworks. The first framework can be called the *mutual influence orientation,* which assumes that communication properties begin to emerge only at the two-person (dyadic) or greater level.[5] Furthermore, meaning is assumed to be created not *within* a given individual but rather *between* individuals. The second framework can be called the *cognitive orientation,* which views each person as an information processor capable of handling social (relational) information as one aspect of thinking and reasoning.[6] Within this framework, meaning is assumed to rest *within* the individual rather than *between* individuals.

DEVELOPING A DESCRIPTIVE BASE

An examination of communication in relationships within both of these frameworks will lead researchers to study a wide variety of relationships: friendship, marriage, parenthood, and love relationships, as well as the relationships formed within working and institutional environments. Preliminary to the development of theories under either the mutual influence or the cognitive orientation, the nature of such relationships must be set forth in greater descriptive detail.

Relationships can be described in detail through taxonomies. A taxonomy describes all the important dimensions of relationships and specifies rules as to how a given relationship can be categorized.[7] We anticipate extensive taxonomical work in the 80's to isolate the dimensions and types of ongoing relationships. The descriptive techniques utilized will include not only empirically derived, statistically validated classification systems of relationships but also simple phenomenological descriptions by participants of their communicative exchanges. The most comprehensive research of the 80's will merge the participants' perspectives and the more empirical measures to describe how individuals organize their ongoing relationships.

While the communication processes and the outcomes of various types of relationships will be studied, there will be extensive interest in the study of families and friendships. Both the mutual influence and the cognitive orientations will be utilized to examine communication in these two types of relationships. The next section outlines some directions that may be taken, and some problems that may be encountered, in applying the mutual influence approach.

APPLYING THE MUTUAL INFLUENCE ORIENTATION

The mutual influence orientation defines communication as a process in which individuals are simultaneously influencing and influenced by one another. Therefore, the meaning of a communicative act does not reside in the occurrence of a given act but in the relationship of acts to one another and their sequence. Using this approach, the observation that Paul speaks more often than Mary is less significant than the observation that Paul speaks more often than Mary after Julie interrupts him. To date our research on relationships has rarely incorporated a conceptualization of the communication process as one of mutual influence. This will be rectified in the 80's.

Examining the mutual influences that occur in a family system, researchers in the 80's will be confronted with two decisions.[8] The first decision is whether the dyad (two-person subsystem) or a larger group should be the unit of analysis. The second decision involves the determination of what constitutes a communication sequence. These decisions will define the boundaries of family communication systems.

It is expected that researchers will proceed by treating complex systems in terms of their dyadic components.[9] While there has been some attention paid to the marital dyad, few of the other dyadic components of the family system, such as parent–child or sibling–sibling, have been examined. Unfortunately, the role of the child has been largely neglected in our research on communication in families. With the growing realization that children influence marital and family interaction, even as they are socialized and influenced by that interaction, the role of children will be addressed more frequently in the 80's.

In utilizing this model to study family communication, much of the emphasis has been placed on studying the control aspects of messages. Researchers in the 80's should consider not only other subsystems within the family but also other concepts within this theoretical approach. A wealth of information awaits communication scholars who will consider concepts such as redundancy, channel disjunctiveness, disconfirmation, punctuation, metacommunication, and homeostasis. In addition, serious attention needs to be given to those positive feedback processes that allow the system to cope with change as well as the more usually studied[10] negative ones that keep the system in balance.

Obviously, significant interpersonal relationships also exist outside the context of the family. The plethora of studies during the 60's and 70's on initial attraction between strangers did not yield much information about communication in relationships. Consequently, the field will turn increasingly to the study of the initiation, maintenance, and disintegration of intimacy.[11] Theory will evolve in the direction of developmental models that consider the life history of relationships. We currently know very little about adult, voluntary, social relationships, although the maintenance of friendships is emerging as a major concern in modern life. As a result, research will not be limited to the study of marital dyads or families (or even dyads en route to family formation) as communication studies will increasingly focus on friendship.

The examination of families and friendships will be brought together in an attempt to map relationships onto the wider social networks in which they are embedded. The influence of the social environment on a dyad and its development and/or disintegration is extensive, although our current knowledge of this process in meager.[12] Information about the social and personal networks of dyadic partners and family members will be sought in the 80's because it will reveal much about the nature of communication in these relationships.

APPLYING THE COGNITIVE ORIENTATION

Our textbooks in communication often exhort us to remember that "meanings are in people." Very little of our research effort has been directed to exploring this aphorism in great detail. Interest in the 80's will return to an examination of the individual and the way that s/he assigns meaning to interpersonal events. An adequate analysis of communication must give serious attention to the cognitive processes of the individual interactants.

Studies of how individuals in ongoing relationships assign meaning to messages will be influenced by the work currently being done in the emerging interdisciplinary field of cognitive science. Drawing on this work, three approaches to the study of meaning seem especially promising. The first involves the development of a communication-based attribution theory. In its broadest sense, attribution theory deals with how we come to understand the causes and implications of the events we witness and participate in—that is, how we assign meaning to the behavior of ourselves and others. A communication-based attribution theory will be especially useful in delineating the sources of bias and error as individuals assign meaning to communication behavior.[13]

A second cognitive approach is the study of what individuals actually say to one another. As we have seen in the 70's the purely formal study of language per se is not going to help us understand interpersonal communication. What we need to uncover is how much information an individual has to have about her or his conversational partner in order to communicate. An important issue for the 80's will be how such information is represented in an individual's cognitive system and how this information is acquired and used in the comprehension and production of messages.[14]

A third approach considers how individuals categorize, simplify, and process information when making social judgments about others. This process of making judgments about others often involves the creation of implicit theories concerning another's personality and/or communication. In the 80's the study of these implicit theories will concentrate on both the relationships that a perceiver sees among the attributes believed to be possessed by another and the person categories that a perceiver generates in order to communicate with others.[15]

Within the cognitive orientation, the study of interpersonal communication in the 80's will focus on how individuals in relationships attribute causes to the behaviors and responses of themselves and their partners, how they comprehend the conversations in which they engage, and how they develop implicit theories of communication and relationships. All of these approaches are individualistic in that they focus on meaning from the perspective of the social actor.

SUMMARY

These predictions of research directions in the 1980's may be viewed as too conservative, stressing as they do merely incremental changes in the way that we study interpersonal phenomena. Indeed, they are conservative insofar as they predict a return to consideration of one of the classic questions for scholars and teachers of communication: What is the nature of meaning? The predictions are more forward-looking, however, in that they suggest that meaning will be considered in a number of different relational contexts and from a variety of different theoretical perspectives.

The implications of these predictions for the teaching of interpersonal communication are relatively straightforward. Courses will need to be developed at all educational levels that focus on both relational and family communication. These courses will have to be structured to take into account the different meanings that specific messages, attitudes, and behaviors may hold for different relationships.

Each of our courses must incorporate a recognition of the cognitive processes of communicators. We will all learn from cognitive science the limitations on how much and what kind of information can be stored and retrieved by the human processor.[16] These findings can help us to set guidelines for generating messages intended to be understood and retained. Attribution-training games will be developed to help students uncover the sources of their attributional biases and errors. Our courses will examine how the impressions, beliefs, theories, or schemas that individuals hold about one another can be modified. We will need to teach what properties of the message can change cognitions. The 80's will see a coming of age of the field of interpersonal communication. By concentrating on the core question of meaning and by pursuing research in that domain, we can participate in an area of communication that promises to be exciting and revitalizing.[17]

REFERENCES

1. Miller, Gerald R., and Burgoon, Michael. "Persuasion Research: Review and Commentary." *Communication Yearbook II.* (Edited by Brent D. Ruben.) New Brunswick, N.J.: Transaction–I.C.A., 1978. pp. 29–47.

2. Fitzpatrick, Mary Anne, and Winke, Jeffrey. "You Always Hurt the One You Love: Strategies and Tactics in Interpersonal Conflict." *Communication Quarterly* 27: 3–11; 1979.

3. Byrne, Donn. Informal remarks at a program entitled "Interpersonal Communication Behavior: Theoretical Perspectives" during the annual meeting of the Speech Communication Association, San Francisco, December 27–30, 1976.

4. Cappella, Joseph. "Communication Theory." Unpublished course syllabus, University of Wisconsin, 1979.

5. See, for example: Watzlawick, Paul; Beavin, Janet H.; and Jackson, Don D. *Pragmatics of Human Communication.* New York: Norton, 1967.

Courtwright, John A.; Millar, Frank E.; and Rogers-Millar, L. Edna. "Domineeringness and Dominance: Replication and Extension." *Communication Monographs* 46: 179–192; 1979.

Millar, Frank E.; Rogers-Millar, L. Edna; and Courtwright, John A. "Relational Control and Dyadic Understanding: An Exploratory Predictive Regression Model." *Communication Yearbook III.* (Edited by Dan Nimmo.) New Brunswick, N.J.: Transaction–I.C.A., 1979. pp. 213–224.

Millar, Frank E., and Rogers, L. Edna. "A Relational Approach to Interpersonal Communication." *Explorations in Interpersonal Communication.* (Edited by Gerald R. Miller.) Beverly Hills, Calif.: Sage, 1976. pp. 87–104.

Rogers, L. Edna, and Farace, Richard V. "An Analysis of Relational Communication in Dyads: New Measurement Procedures." *Human Communication Research* 1: 222–239; 1975.

6. See, for example: Craig, Robert T. "Information Systems Theory and Research: An Overview of Individual Information Processing." *Communication Yearbook III.* (Edited by Dan Nimmo.) New Brunswick, N.J.: Transaction–I.C.A., 1979. pp. 99–122.

Planap, Sally, and Tracy, Karen. "Not to Change the Topic But . . . : A Cognitive Approach to the Management of Conversation." *Communication Yearbook IV.* (Edited by Dan Nimmo.) New Brunswick, N.J.: Transaction–I.C.A., in press.

7. Fitzpatrick, Mary Anne. *A Typological Approach to Communication in Enduring Relationships.* Dissertation. Philadelphia: Temple University, 1976. (Unpublished)

8. Parke, Ross D.; Power, Thomas G.; and Gottman, John M. "Conceptualizing and Quantifying Influence Patterns in the Family Triad." *Social Interaction Analysis.* (Edited by M.E. Lamb, S.J. Suomi, and G.R. Stephenson.) Madison: University of Wisconsin Press, 1979. pp. 231–252.

9. Consider, for example, a six-person family. It would include 15 dyads, 20 triads, 15 quadrads, and 6 five-person groups. Even explaining the interaction in the family system in terms of component dyads would be a complex task.

10. Very little mention is made in this review of the concept of *affect.* Affect is not generally discussed in the "new communication theory" models because it is considered an individual-level variable. Affect can be conceptualized as a mutual influence process, and some steps have been made in that direction. See, for example: Gottman, John M.; Markman, Howard; and Notarius, Clifford. "The Topography of Marital Conflict: A Study of Verbal and Nonverbal Behavior." *Journal of Marriage and the Family* 39: 461–477; 1977.

11. Levinger, George, and Raush, Harold L. *Close Relationships: Perspectives on the Meaning of Intimacy.* Amherst: University of Massachusetts Press, 1977.

12. Burgess, Robert, and Huston, Ted. *Social Exchange in Developing Relationships.* New York: Academic Press, 1979.

13. See, for example: Ross, Lee. "The Intuitive Psychologist and His Shortcomings: Distortions in the Attribution Process." *Advances in Experimental Social Psychology.* (Edited by Leonard Berkowitz.) New York: Academic Press, 1977. Vol. 10, pp. 173–220.

Ross, Lee. "Some Afterthoughts on the Intuitive Psychologist." *Cognitive Theories in Social Psychology.* (Edited by Leonard Berkowitz.) New York: Academic Press, 1978. pp. 385–400.

Sillars, Alan L. *Communication and Attributions in Interpersonal Conflict.* Dissertation. Madison: University of Wisconsin, 1980. (Unpublished)

14. See, for example: Johnson-Laird, Phillip, and Wason, Peter C. *Thinking: Readings in Cognitive Science.* Cambridge, England: Cambridge University Press, 1977. Also, articles published in the journal *Discourse Processes.*

15. See, for example: Rands, Marilyn, and Levinger, George. "Implicit Theories of Relationship: An Intergenerational Study." *Journal of Personality and Social Psychology* 37: 645–661; 1979.

Cantor, Nancy, and Mischel, Walter. "Prototypes in Person Perception." *Advances in Experimental Social Psychology.* (Edited by Leonard Berkowitz.) New York: Academic Press, in press. Vol. 12.

Ebbesen, Ebbe B., and Allen, Robert B. "Cognitive Processes in Implicit Personality Trait Inference." *Journal of Personality and Social Psychology* 37: 471–488; 1979.

Rosenberg, Seymour, and Sedlak, Andrea. "Structural Representations of Implicit Personality Theory." *Advances in Experimental Social Psychology.* (Edited by Leonard Berkowitz.) New York: Academic Press, 1972. Vol. 10, pp. 174–226.

Schneider, David J. "Implicit Personality Theory: A Review." *Psychological Bulletin* 79: 294–309; 1973.

16. See, for example: Norman, Donald A., and Bobrow, Daniel G. "On the Economy Side of the Human Processing System." *Psychological Review* 86: 214–255; 1979.

17. The author is grateful to Julie Indvik for her helpful criticisms of earlier drafts of this chapter.

Additional Readings

Burgess, Robert I., and Huston, Ted, editors. *Social Exchange in Developing Relationships.* New York: Academic Press, 1979. Examining relationships from a social exchange framework, this book contains a number of excellent articles on how social exchange models can be used to trace the growth and development of interpersonal relationships. The book takes some new looks at relational initiation and conflict in relationships as well as the potential exchange relationship between the dyad and its larger social network.

Hastie, R., and others, editors. *Person Memory: The Cognitive Basis of Social Perception.* Hillsdale, N.J.: Lawrence Erlbaum, 1980. The basic concern of this book is how we represent social information in memory. The introductory chapter outlines how we can develop an adequate account of the perception, retention, and eventual utilization of the information we have about others. This book uses findings in the study of cognition to examine social behavior.

Higgins, E. Tory; Herman, C. Peter; and Zanna, Mark P., editors. *Social Cognition.* Hillsdale, N.J.: Lawrence Erlbaum, 1980. The authors in this volume examine important issues in how we process and store social information about others. The book includes some ideas on how we make inferences about another's personality; how we form, maintain, and change initial impressions; and how we manage our own impressions, both verbally and nonverbally.

Knapp, Mark. *Social Intercourse: From Greeting to Goodbye.* Boston: Allyn and Bacon, 1978. This book takes a developmental perspective of the study of interpersonal relationships. The major strength lies in the specification of communication behaviors at each relationship stage from the initiation of a relationship to its termination. The book contains a number of interesting examples and hypotheses about communication in relationships.

Lerner, Richard M., and Spanier, Graham B. *Child Influences on Marital and Family Interaction.* New York: Academic Press, 1978. This book contains 12 essays that examine parent–

child interactions from a variety of perspectives. Its particular strength lies in its treatment of the parent–child relationship across the life span. Rather than adhering to older conceptions of parents influencing children or children influencing parents, this book sees the parent–child relationship as a dynamic, reciprocal one with parents and children exerting mutual influence on one another.

Levinger, George, and Raush, Harold, editors. *Close Relationships: Perspectives on the Meaning of Intimacy.* Amherst: University of Massachusetts Press, 1977. This book is a collection of essays on close relationships. Beginning with a discussion of how the meaning assigned to relationships has changed through history, the book touches on such issues as commitment, interdependence, stability, satisfaction, and a number of other issues related to pair bonding.

CHAPTER 10

Issues in Education on
Mass Communication in the 80's

Peter V. Miller
Content Consultants: Peter Clark
University of Michigan
F. Gerald Kline
University of Minnesota

At the end of the 1950's, C. Wright Mills slashed at contemporary, empirical social science research on mass communication for its lack of historical perspective.[1] One cannot understand the phenomenon of mass *communication,* he contended, without reference to the emergence of mass *society* during the nineteenth and twentieth centuries. For individuals, the mass society argument goes, the transformation of feudal societies into nation states meant a dislocation from traditional group ties —extended family, church, and the like—and a reorganization of social life in huge conglomerations of disaffected, isolated beings. The matrix bonding society became the standardized popular culture symbols conveyed by the mass media—organizations that began to flourish with the growth of industrialization and urbanization. Controllers of the media could, and did, manipulate the "atomized" mass audience for profit or status.

This view of media roles and power has not gone unchallenged in the years since Mills wrote. The empirical rejoinder to his critique is that modern society retains qualities of pluralism that it inherited from feudalism. Primary group life is said to prosper, and it has formed the basis for selectivity in cultural taste and political attitudes, which blunted the impact of mass communicated messages. Rather than a hapless collection of persuasible individuals, the audiences for mass media fare are argued to be active, tenacious defenders of their parochial viewpoints. The mass media might inform, but they could not persuade.

During the 1980's the debate over whether the mass media are all-powerful manipulators of masses or simply brokers of symbols to suspicious consumers will be complicated by developments that will lead us to question whether the media are really "mass" at all. Changes in the organization of media industries, in technology, and possibly in regulation may render the debate between mass society theorists and empirical social scientists obsolete.

Indeed, there is a case to be made that several of the media that we normally group under the heading "mass" really do not belong there. Newspapers, radio, film, and magazines all structure their content to appeal to *particular* segments of society, rather than trying to attract diverse demographic or taste groups. Thus, while their audiences can number in the millions, the sociological character of the audiences belies the status of mass media for these purveyors of information and entertainment.

This leaves television as our only truly mass medium. It is often said that radio, film, and magazines adapted to the presence of television by taking on their present diversified forms. Unable to compete with television for the mass audience, network radio programs, general audience films, and *Life* and *Look* Magazines were culled from the mass media through a process of "natural selection." The content remaining in these media was more finely tuned to appeal to a great variety of taste subcultures. A radio listener of 40 years ago would not have envisioned the airwaves crowded with "Easy Listening," "Country and Western," and "Top 40" programming, to name a few of the more popular formats. A reader of *Life* during that time would not have anticipated the success of *Runner's World*—a vivid example of profitable segmentation in the magazine industry. Newspapers, while never truly a "mass" medium because of their local orientation, are now becoming more like magazines in offering independent special content sections. The "Darwinian" explanation for all of these changes emphasizes the need for media to adapt new forms to survive in the hostile environment created by television.

But the 1980's are likely to see some marked changes in television itself. Depending on how rapidly various technological innovations see widespread adoption, the well-known three-network organizational structure for the medium may be supplanted by a much more diversified arrangement. These innovations include more penetration of cable television into markets across the country, the combination of satellite relays and cable to form new networking arrangements, "instant" networks created among independent stations carrying packages of special content (sports and miniseries), increases in over-air pay television, and extended allocation of portions of the UHF spectrum for new broadcasting stations. These developments, singly and in combination, could have the effect of "demassifying" our only mass medium by providing an ever-broader range of content offerings that will appeal to specific segments of the audience.

At the same time the financial base of television would be altered because mass advertising would be replaced by commercials tailored to sports, drama, or comedy audiences, for example—that is, unless advertising support is eliminated entirely as it has been in various pay television schemes. Many cable franchises now offer movie packages or features like Home Box Office that have programming uninterrupted by commercials.

Rather than three national networks, satellite technology makes possible the linking of cable outlets and VHF or UHF stations in "networks" for a single program or for longer periods of time. Independent UHF stations, once the "poor cousins" of the industry, are now envied for their profits from "instant networking" arrangements for sports or miniseries telecasts. Home video cassette recorders, "teletext," and video discs add yet a further element of segmentation, as viewers have even more opportunity to substitute their chosen content for network fare. These developments point to the possibility that television will go the way of its predecessors in seeking to take advantage of the wide variety in tastes hidden in the mass audience.

Predictions like this are common, and have been made in earlier decades. The appeal of diversified content has not always been great enough to warrant the capital investment required to provide it, and technology does not always develop as quickly as its advocates predict. But the success of a number of such investments and a more laissez faire regulatory environment are leading to an accelerated pace of development.

The attempts in Congress to draft a new Communications Act (to replace the one passed in 1934) suggest a more libertarian view toward television and radio regulation, as does recent policy promulgated by the Federal Communications Commission toward cable television. Once prohibited from certain markets because of the alleged threat to the profitability of local UHF stations, cable is now recognized as an aid to those channels because of the better signal quality provided to subscribers. Other restrictive attitudes toward cable and pay TV are also changing. Allocation of channels in the radio and UHF spectrum, once thought to be determined absolutely by the limitations of the airwaves in handling signals, is now thought to be less constrained by this factor, and new broadcast stations may be authorized as a result—leading (perhaps) to more diversity in content.

These trends toward greater segmentation of the various media audiences have marked implications for education about mass communication in the future. Tracing the progress of the changes is itself a subject of primary importance. Students of communication should be among the most astute observers of patterns of development across media industries and of government–media relationships.

The new content that may become available to consumers through changes in the industry holds the promise of raising cultural standards and providing citizens with more in-depth information than is currently available. The rub, as F. Gerald Kline has pointed out, is that consumers must *choose* to be exposed to the material that is offered. Part of the job of instructors concerned with mass communication is simply to explain to students the impact of channel diversity on content. Instructors should also encourage a wide exposure to various viewpoints and types of entertainment, assuming that a broad range of viewpoints is better than a narrow one. It was eloquently expressed by Milton in *Areopagitica* —his apologia for freedom of expression—in which he argued that if Truth is in the field contending with many other viewpoints, it will prevail. If this notion has any validity, it requires public awareness of all sides on an issue. More broadly construed, if we are to have a common ground for discourse in cultural or political matters, each individual must be exposed to a good sampling of the wide range of content available in the newly reorganized media. If audiences merely attend to their preferred entertainment and points of view, the benefits of diversity will be lost in the parochialism of choice. A central task for teachers, at whatever level of education, is to instill a tolerance for opposing viewpoints and an appreciation for alternative cultural forms. The adaptation of audiences to the new offerings will be a primary focus for research and education as well.

The "demassification" of the mass audience, to the extent it occurs, is likely to lead to a different sort of social criticism of the media. Television, the scapegoat of critics for many years, has held that position largely because of its organizational structure. If television programming becomes more segmented, its vaunted power as a shaper of opinions and behavior will be diminished. Paul Hirsch has pointed out that when radio and film were once the mass media, they were subject to the same sorts of criticism as television.[2] Since the change in their audience compositions, critics have turned their attention to the medium that has standardized content meant for everyone. Concern about television aggression, sexual portrayal, advertising, and the like will be quieted as more types of content become available on that medium. The research agenda will change to complement the shift in social concern.

Another "freedom of expression" issue for the 1980's will be the evolving relationship between the press and the Supreme Court. The Burger court has issued several rulings that seem to restrict the freedom of the press in reporting on trials, and has authorized the use of search warrants in newsrooms by prosecutors searching for evidence in criminal proceedings. Gag orders on the reporting of trials are becoming more common, and reporters' notes are more likely to be the object of subpoenas unless the "chilling effect" of such actions leads to a decline in investigative reporting. The press, which enjoyed a felicitous environment during the time of the Warren court, has complained bitterly about the new attitude among the current Justices, and the Court itself has become the subject of a chatty investigative reporting job.

Mass communication research paid much attention to violence in the 1960's and to advertising effects in the 1970's. Politics forms a subject matter of continual interest. Much of mass communication research in the last two decades has looked at the effects of media content on young people. Stereotypes of various groups on television were also the subject of much research in the 1970's. We should see greater attention paid to media and aging in the 80's with the gradual shift of population to the upper end of the age continuum. Energy and foreign affairs information is likely to be a primary focus of research as well because these issues will be particularly pressing during the 80's. The consequences of energy problems for the media themselves will bear watching since energy shortages are bound to change the cost structure of media products. Newspapers are already responding regularly to steadily climbing newsprint costs.

In summary, the 1980's are likely to be years of diversification in the mass media, with consequent changes in the content offered and researchers' attention to media effects. More and more individual choice in the use of media will become possible. The choice may lead to a better-informed society—or to a fragmented one. The benefits and costs of "freedom of expression" are issues that will form the basis of debate about the mass media in this decade.

REFERENCES

1. Mills, C. Wright. *Sociological Imagination.* New York: Oxford University Press, 1959.

2. Hirsch, Paul. "Television As a National Medium: Its Cultural and Political Role in American Society." *Handbook of Urban Life.* (Edited by David Street.) San Francisco: Jossey-Bass, 1977.

Additional Readings

Carey, James, and Miller, Peter, editors. *Sage Annual Reviews of Communication Research.* Beverly Hills, Calif.: Sage Publications, Inc. Vols. 1, 2, 3, 4, 6, 7, 9, and 10 of this series, formerly edited by F. Gerald Kline and Peter Clarke, concerned (and will concern) various aspects of mass communication and communication research methods. Among the topics addressed are political communication, news organizations, content analysis, and media audiences' uses and gratifications.

Comstock, George, and others. *Television and Human Behavior.* New York: Columbia University Press, 1978. A wide-ranging review of findings on the effects of television content on audiences.

Robinson, Glen, editor. *Communications for Tomorrow: Policy Perspectives for the 1980s.* New York: Aspen Institute for Humanistic Studies, 1978. A collection of articles on media regulation, industry structure, and technology.

CHAPTER 11

Teaching Interpretation in the 80's

Lee Hudson
Beverly Whitaker Long
Content Consultants: Paul H. Gray
University of Texas at Austin
Mary Frances Hopkins
Louisiana State University—Baton Rouge

If we predated this essay to focus on the early 1930's, we could settle into a discussion of the "oral interpretation of literature" and its fairly recent name change from "oral expression" and the "vocal interpretation of literature." We would enjoy the comforts of a generally widespread consensus on what oral interpretation or interpretative reading should accomplish and how. Interpretation, then well-flanked by the aesthetics of conventions, could handily be defined either by what it was (the re-creation and communication of literature) or by what it was not (acting, impersonation, and public speaking). The last 50 years, however, have seen these particular determinants steadily fade. To investigate this large shift in perspective, we will proceed from a brief historical overview to an outline of current theory and practice, suggesting implications for education in the 80's. We will, through this general terrain, pursue the thesis that as speech communication struggles to align its humanistic heritage with its current pragmatism, the 80's will be a pivotal decade for interpretation. (In this essay we use the words *interpretation* and *performance* interchangeably although a distinction can be made between interpretation as a perspective and performance as a perspective rendered.

THE AMERICAN TRADITION OF INTERPRETATION

When the National Association of Academic Teachers of Public Speaking was formed in 1914, the elocutionary influence on public address and oral reading began to slowly dissolve. The earlier-formulated expression theory emerged with an insistence that the *internal* realization of literature govern its *external* presentation, supplanting the elocutionist's frequent reverse emphasis on proper delivery techniques. Guided by an aesthetic of minimalism or suggestion, readers could, thus, share literature with others while simultaneously developing their own inner resources. The second two decades of the century were not literature-oriented times, but rather, in their own divergent ways, both insisted on the performer's physical, mental, or spiritual growth, and literature provided a more or less satisfactory vehicle for this improvement.

While some serious consideration of the literature did exist earlier among a few writers, the 30's and 40's brought rationales grounded in literary theory for reading and its communication to others. Interpretation began what was to become a pattern up to the present day—the application of methods current in literary criticism to the students' purpose for oral reading and their preparation of materials. In the 40's that methodology was not as consistent as it would be later. As yet, readers still wrote a precis or paraphrase of the selection in a general search for the author's central meaning—a practice soon to fall under the heavy fire of the New Critics who provided vocabulary and a method for examining the specifics of a literary text.

In the 50's interpretation educators voiced dissatisfaction with the terms *readings* and *recitations,* and with the lifeless, unintelligent renderings these descriptors implied. Instead, they developed a fuller conceptualization of interpretation, one that considered performances as critical explorations or textual illuminations of a literary selection. It was a short, but crucial, step to then view the performance itself as a demonstrated act of literary criticism offering unique critical insight. Performance as criticism combined the detachment of an objective, analytical, critical method with the engagement inherent in a performer's directly experiential approach. *Performance as knowing* became the key concept dominating, in one way or another, the contributions made during the 60's. An important transition was just beginning: Presentation, oral reading, representation, expression, recitation, or interpretation was evolving into the fuller concept of *performed literature.* Probably because it conjured up thoughts of trivial activity, impersonation, or acting, the word *performance* did not popularly, or even casually, appear in interpretation literature until the 1960's. Diversity within the field was identifiable as teachers began developing their areas of emphasis: the *reader's* growth (technically as a performer or humanistically as a person); the *audience's* understanding and enjoyment of the shared literature; or the study of *literature* through the medium of performance.

The late 60's and the 70's added the dynamics of the concept of performance to the textual implications of New Criticism. Instead of criticism's leading a reader from understanding to presenting, performance was insisting on its simultaneous textual ontology: The text *was* its performance. With each performance the literature was being redefined. The meaning of *performance* in its basic sense—to bring a thing to completion—reminds us that to comprehend is to perform, in a sense. We perform when we realize, recognize, and understand the integrated emotional and cognitive dimensions of the literary text. A vocal–physical–psychical performance, then, expands to encompass our sense of all three contexts—social, literary, and personal. Naturally a public performance will involve a social sensibility conditioned by audience identity and purpose. The literary context introduces consideration of both the literary speaker's audience and the author's historical audience. A personal context, in addition, governs the development of a student's highly individual encounter with literature.

THEORY AND PRACTICE FOR THE 1980'S

With neither crystal ball nor prophetic powers to spin out developments in the teaching of interpretation in the 80's, we can only examine the salient strengths of the present and outline what is likely to happen, to continue, or to intensify if educators persist in believing—as we think they will—that performance is a challenging and worthwhile way of studying literature. The items we will comment on include basic philosophical objectives and the movement of performance from the speech communication classroom to other settings.

Basic Philosophical Objectives

The basic objective of performance as literary study is closely tied to the root meaning of the word *perform:* execute, fulfill, complete, furnish, finish. In each case, the lower life synonym is simply *do.* And why this "doing" of literature? The reason lies in the interest of knowing or, better still, in a knowing/feeling of those experiences expressed in literary texts. Such a thesis claims that performance, central to the whole literary process, is more fully realized if the reader actually "tries on" what the literature notates by performing it (doing, actualizing, acting, being, etc.).

Louise Rosenblatt, a noted English educator, claims that a written piece of literature is a *text* and that a *poem* (or any literature) exists only as a transaction occurs between *reader* and text.[1] The print on the page, thus, becomes an experience in literature only when a person—or persons—makes connection with it.

If an even more basic goal is needed, we can borrow one from Walter Ong, S.J., who writes: "Acting a role, realizing in a specially intense way one's identity (in a sense) with someone who (in another sense) one is not, remains one of the most human things a person can do."[2] The potential liberalizing effect of this "realizing in a specially intense way" is not yet scientifically measurable; however, it is a firmly held commitment (and one that is confirmed almost daily) for most teachers and students of liberal and performing arts, and the conviction seems likely to grow even more secure in the 80's.

Performance in Special Situations

Even for those who find the raison d'être for interpretation in its value to literary study, the time comes when teachers have an opportunity to take performing techniques and/or performances outside their own classroom for different or wider audiences. The most common example occurs when the teacher's aims move from the literary growth of the individual through the *process* of performance to an interest in performance as *product* for the understanding and enjoyment of an audience. Ordinarily labeled readers' theatre or chamber theatre, these group performances face most of the same problems as do other theatrical events: a playing space, adequate facilities, budget, copyright, programs, costumes, etc. Although these performances are not generally expected to be as lavish as traditional theatre (largely because the Aristotelian element of "spectacle" is rarely emphasized or even attempted), the teacher still faces responsibility for ensuring the audience, insofar as possible, an aesthetically engaging and satisfying time in the theatre. Inadequately prepared theatre, regardless of its label, is only minimally educational. Certainly not meant to discourage public performances by interpreters, this assertion is intended only to suggest that enterprises appropriate to the classroom may disappoint public audiences who have reason to expect a finished and carefully honed production, the kind implicitly promised by the invitation or advertisement. Interpretation teachers' effectiveness may be greatly strengthened by training in theatre and allied arts; their directing of productions demands it, formally or informally.

91

Another kind of performance outside the classroom now enjoying a resurgence in popularity occurs in specialized social contexts: prisons, hospitals, recreation centers, retirement homes, and discussion groups, for example. Used as entertainment or as illustrative material for lecture–discussions led by an expert, these performances can be meaningful for performers and listeners.

Teachers interested in performance as a service to other groups should look for opportunities within their own school system: having reading hours to promote library week; giving dramatized readings of famous debates for a history course; reading poems for elementary school children who are interested in composing their own; and performing innumerable selections for English classes about to begin a given unit of study.

A less obvious connection just starting to be explored also occurs in English classrooms, but with a decidedly different emphasis (and one that is especially exciting for the teacher of speech communication). As a result of the important studies made by the National Council of Teachers of English in the late 60's, English education programs have been exploring ways in which solo performances in class, oral reading exercises, and group interpretation activities enhance student understanding and enjoyment of literature. Most recently, reading acquisition and composition programs have been investigating the influence of performance behaviors on written communication competency. If we absorb the vocabulary, grammar, and rhythms of language through speech (initially in childhood and throughout life), then oralizing and internalizing expressive language from our literature in a performance situation could well extend our language sensibilities and usage. Thus, interpretation teachers may be centrally involved in the return of joint programs in oral and written English.

CONCLUSION

In the introduction to this chapter we speculated that the 80's would be a pivotal decade as speech communication attempts to align its humanistic heritage with its current pragmatism. The ensuing discussion reveals our commitment, first and foremost, to the humanistic impulse—in the belief that here is where interpretation most properly can make a major contribution to students whose present and future lives may be significantly enriched by full encounters with literature. Moreover, of the speech communication arts and sciences, interpretation is, perhaps, the most humanistically oriented and, thus, able to make important and unique contributions to the field of speech communication as a whole.

In short, we affirm the humanness, even the naturalness, of literary study and the possibilities of insight through literature in performance. Literature, both on the page and in performance, merits our students' careful attention—even what Richard McGuire calls *passionate* attention. In the introduction to *Passionate Attention: An Introduction to Literary Study*, he explains:

> I see the acts of living and of reading and studying literature as having value only if they are motivated by love and interest; passionate attention is thus the richest short description of literary criticism I know. It represents the most important human qualities involved in a person's relationships with other persons and with literature.[3]

If we add to his acts "of living . . . reading and studying literature" the acts of attending to performances in and of texts, we may say with him that "passionate attention" is the "richest short description" available for what we envision for the performance of literature in the 80's—and beyond.

REFERENCES

1. Rosenblatt, Louise. *The Reader, The Text, The Poem: The Transactional Theory of the Literary Work.* Carbondale: Southern Illinois University Press, 1978.

2. Ong, Walter, S.J., as cited in: Gibson, Walker. *Persona: A Style Study for Readers and Writers.* New York: Random House, 1968.

3. McGuire, Richard. *Passionate Attention: An Introduction to Literary Study.* New York: W.W. Norton, 1973.

Additional Readings

Bacon, Wallace A. *The Art of Interpretation.* Third edition. New York: Holt, Rinehart and Winston, 1979.

_____, and Breen, Robert. *Literature as Experience.* New York: McGraw-Hill, 1959.

Beloof, Robert L. *The Performing Voice in Literature.* Boston: Little, Brown, and Co., 1966.

Doyle, Esther M., and Floyd, Virginia Hastings. *Studies in Interpretation.* Amsterdam: Rodopi NV, Vol. I—1972, Vol. II—1978.

Geiger, Don. *The Sound, Sense, and Performance of Literature.* Chicago: Scott, Foresman and Co., 1963.

Roloff, Leland H. *The Perception and Evocation of Literature.* Glenview, Ill.: Scott, Foresman and Co., 1973.

CHAPTER 12

Organizational Communication in the 80's: The Complications of Cooperation

Bonnie McD. Johnson
Content Consultants: Sue DeWine
Ohio University
Raymond L. Falcione
University of Maryland

"What is organizational communication?" I am often asked this by students, friends, people on airplanes, and my mother. The possible answers to that question are as varied as the people who are in the field. This chapter is about what those people do. Most simply, to "do" organizational communication is to use your communication (to create, exchange, and interpret symbolic messages) in order to cooperate (to work together). Organizational communication has become a vocation only relatively recently. It has emerged as a specialized field of activity and research because people are increasingly recognizing that cooperation is *problematic:* Organization of work is difficult to accomplish. Moreover, the kinds of symbols people exchange have an important impact on the effectiveness of their cooperation. At one time people could take communication and its role in cooperation for granted, but as cooperation becomes more complicated, people are increasingly turning their attention to investigating how to improve cooperation by improving communication.

Let us examine cooperation, communication, and the impact of complication as an introduction to the direction of organizational communication in the 1980's. Consider two 10-year-olds working together to construct a model rocket. They are "doing" organizational communication at its most basic level. Their actions constitute the simplest kind of cooperative system. The most basic question that can be asked in the study of organizational communication is this: How are such simple systems of cooperation accomplished? In this simplest cooperative system, communication researchers would study the words exchanged by the model builders, their nonverbal messages, the words and form of the written instructions they are following, and even the setting of their activities (e.g., whether they have suitable chairs and a table or whether they are sitting on the floor). Communication researchers ask how the two model builders use symbols to construct similar meanings for what they are doing (for example, how to apply paint) and how they construct expectations about what each is to do (for example, that he will apply glue and that she will assemble parts).[1]

Now, let us consider the complications necessary to transform the basic cooperative system created by these 10-year-old model rocket builders into the national effort to explore space carried out by the National Aeronautics and Space Administration (NASA).[2] Let us take some of the major "complications" added to a simple cooperative system, and consider how an organizational communication researcher might study the use of symbolic messages in creating human cooperative systems and what kinds of activities might be done by those who specialize in the "doing" of organizational communication. The complications we shall examine are these:

1. Add 100,000 people.

2. Create differences in authority.

3. Add many years to the work.

4. Create uncertainty about the work to be done.

5. Require billions of dollars to finance the work.

6. Impose government regulation on the work.

1. *Add 100,000 people.* Most of the people who work in a large organization such as a NASA are strangers to each other; in fact, each will not be able to see many of the others or even talk frequently over the phone to more than a few. Simple agreements used by the 10-year-olds, such as "Let's meet at my house at 5:00" and "You glue and I'll stick them together," become complicated into *control subsystems,* specifying all the tasks that need to be done, when, in what order, and by whom.

A control subsystem consists of all those messages people use to know what they are to do, when, how, and why. Some of these messages are transmitted by face-to-face communication, and these may be as simple as the ones the 10-year-olds use. Other messages are written down in official form—for example, job descriptions specifying the minimum expected of each organization position, and procedures manuals detailing how each job is to be done. Some of the most interesting and powerful control messages are implicit or unstated. Much of what a person knows about his or her job is not written down or even spoken; rather, it is in the form of a "routine."

In the 1980's the technology for coordinating the work of thousands of people is going to grow exponentially. Computer-based management information systems have already changed the work routines of people in large organizations. In the next 10 years inexpensive microprocessors will replace the paper work of even small offices. Organizational communication specialists will be examining and directing the effect of new information technologies on organizational control subsystems.

2. *Create differences in authority.* Authority is the right to command another's behavior. If the rocket model belongs equally to the two 10-year-olds, neither may have authority over the other. If it belongs only to her, she has the authority to decide how the work is to be done. He may quit rather than do what he is commanded to do, but both are likely to recognize the general principle that ownership of the means of production—in this case, the rocket kit—gives one the right to say how the work should be done. This right, however, gets complicated when there are many owners, such as when ownership is through stock in a public corporation. There are hundreds of thousands of "owners" of American Telephone and Telegraph, for example. Ownership of public agencies such as NASA is even more widespread. Hence, the simple case of equal or one-sided authority based in ownership becomes complicated into an *authority subsystem* in which people are appointed to have certain rights to direct the actions of others. The most common type of authority subsystem is a hierarchy in which everyone has a supervisor except the person at the very top.

The authority subsystem is a more or less commonly held understanding about who has what right to command. Authority is a characteristic of communication according to Chester I. Barnard, who was for many years chief executive of AT & T; he also at one time headed the National Science Foundation, the USO, the Rockefeller Foundation, and the General Election Board.[3] Even though a person is appointed to a command position by the organization, others will accept his or her message as authoritative (having the right to command their behavior) only when four conditions exist at the time they interpret the message: (1) they understand the message; (2) at the time they believe it to be consistent with the purpose of the organization; (3) at the time they believe it to be generally compatible with their personal interests; (4) they are physically and mentally able to do as commanded. Hence, the executives appointed to command an organization must have especially good communication skills because they work only through communication. Barnard defines the first function of executives as creating and maintaining a system of communication. Although the notion that executive work is communication is not new, in the 1980's we shall witness a renewed interest in the conditions that lead people to interpret a message as authoritative.

3. *Add many years to the work.* The rocket model builders cooperate only as long as it is fun for them, but more complicated organizations need to sustain involvement over long periods of time. This means that people remain part of the cooperative effort even when they would prefer to do something else. Therefore, add to the basic cooperative system an *incentive subsystem,* which will provide each organizational member with something he or she values in exchange for work done for the organization. Thus, the simple feeling of working together because it is pleasurable in itself ("Hey, let's put together my model rocket." "Yeah, that sounds like fun.") becomes complicated into an incentive subsystem of pay, promotion, working conditions, benefits, and even a union to negotiate the terms of agreement to work.

Incentive subsystems operate through symbolic messages: A salary is not simply a payment for services rendered; it is a statement by the organization of how much that person's contribution is worth. Organizational communication specialists of the 1980's will be examining the symbolic dimensions of incentives: What leads people to interpret an organizational message as rewarding?

4. *Create uncertainty about the work to be done.* The 10-year-olds put together a model designed by others. The model kit had a picture of what the finished model would look like and a set of detailed instructions for putting together the model pieces. Much of the knowledge required to build the rocket is provided for anyone who can read and understand the instructions. This would be difficult, perhaps impossible, for a person from another culture who had never seen a rocket model before and, therefore, could not visualize the end product of the work. Even the job of following instructions requires a general understanding of what is to be done—the overall purpose of the cooperation. This vision of purpose, this notion of what happens when, is based on some relevant past experience.

Complicate this relatively simple situation with uncertainty about what the organization's mission is. The vague concept of "build a rocket" must be detailed into a complete design of the rocket and how it can be built. Therefore, add a *research and development* (R&D) *subsystem*. In any organization R&D consists of visualizing the abstract notion of the "organizational mission" into more concrete specifications of what the cooperative system is to create; even organizations such as department stores, where there are no scientists, have jobs that are so complicated that they need people who have specialized training and whose job it is just to think of what might be done and how.

In the 1980's specialized and technical expertise will be increasingly important in cooperation. But specialization makes cooperation difficult. The R&D subsystem consists of work done by people who must know so much about one particular area that they will be virtually ignorant about another. For example, the chemical engineer developing fuel for rockets will have only an elementary understanding of the mechanical engineering principles involved in designing the fuel injection system; yet, chemical engineers and mechanical engineers must cooperate in order to design the overall propulsion of the rocket. Cooperation in such settings is often in the form of conflict. The chemical engineers want the kind of fuel injection system that will allow them to develop the most powerful fuel; yet, that kind of design may be unacceptable to the mechanical engineers because their research indicates that the system will be too heavy or lack dependability.

Uncertainty about what is to be done and how to do it leads to technical specialization in order to increase knowledge and, ultimately, to create better images of what to do. Yet, specialization in knowledge creates conflicts over what is known and what is best to do. R&D people have no authority to command. Rather, they are experts who advise those in authority. Their limited vision results from their organizational position; people with specialized backgrounds who are put in authority positions are required to develop a broader perspective than their previous specialized focus would allow. Specialists in organizational communication in the 1980's will be increasingly called upon to act as translators of technical information for other specialists and for those nonspecialists who ultimately have to make decisions about what is to be done.

5. *Require billions of dollars to finance the work.* Getting the money to buy a rocket kit may be a big problem for the 10-year-olds. Most likely they must convince someone with money to give it to them by persuading the money holder that a benefit will result and that at least some benefit will go to the money holder. ("Mom, if I had a rocket kit, I'd

work quietly in my room today instead of making a lot of noise in the living room.") The benefit of the rocket must be shown to be worth the cost. ("Mom, it would take me twice as long to put together the $6.00 rocket as it would a $4.50 rocket.")

The basic process that is going on here is investment. The more complicated the organization, the more complicated the *subsystem for seeking investment.* Profit-making organizations decide whether they are succeeding or not by using the symbol "return on investment." They make a good return on investment by producing a profit, or a profitable service. Profit-making organizations use communication specialists to convince customers that they will benefit by purchasing what the organization has to sell. In a nonprofit-making organization, the necessity for a return on investment is no less important. For example, people who request funds from the government (through the President's Office of Management and Budget and ultimately through Congress) must persuade the American people's representatives that such an investment will have a worthwhile return. All organizations must sell not only their product but also themselves—their organizational image—to outsiders and also to organizational members. In the 1970's we witnessed an increase in esteem for the "corporate relations" specialist who sells the organizational image. Not only does setting a favorable image lead, in the long run, to more investment but also it leads to a more favorable "regulatory environment." In the 1980's we should see even more emphasis on the importance of specialists in "external communications."

6. *Impose government regulation on the work.*   Even the simplest systems are likely to be regulated by outside authorities. The rocket builders may be "regulated" by their father's insisting that they move their activity to the garage or that they put newspapers under their newly glued pieces. No system of cooperation is without impact on others. The water I use to manufacture a product may pollute your drinking water; the medicine I make for your illness may harm you. Our increasing interdependence and our awareness of the fact that we have no choice but to be interdependent have created an increasing demand for public organizations to regulate other organizations. Therefore, complicate the simplest cooperative system by adding a *regulatory environment* and a *subsystem for coping with regulation.* In the 1980's this environment will have more impact on organizations, and, therefore, the subsystems for coping will be more influential. These subsystems will consist of lawyers and experts in communication.

In coping subsystems, the communication specialists act in several capacities: They teach organization members how to change their behavior to comply (they conduct workshops in interviewing so that selection interviewers know how to ask questions that comply with affirmative action guidelines); they inform organization members about new regulations (they print explanations of new regulations in the newsletter); they lobby with government agencies and legislatures for favorable legislation (Feller and others estimate that about 80 percent of state legislators use lobbyists as important sources of information in considering legislation[4]).

This chapter has described what organizational communication is by describing the activities of those who specialize in "doing" it. Even the simplest organization of cooperation is accomplished through organizational communication. As organizations become more complicated, as they will in the 1980's, there will be an increasing need for those who have an understanding of communication sophisticated enough to take organizational positions in the doing and in the studying of working together.

REFERENCES

1. Johnson, Bonnie McDaniel. *Communication: The Process of Organizing.* Boston: Allyn and Bacon, 1977.

2. This chapter uses NASA only as an illustrative, mostly hypothetical example. For an actual analysis of NASA's organizational communication, see: Tompkins, Phillip K. "Management Qua Communication in Rocket Research and Development." *Communication Monographs* 44: 1–26; March 1977.

Tompkins, Phillip K. "Organizational Metamorphosis in Space Research and Development." *Communication Monographs* 45: 110–118; June 1978.

3. Barnard, Chester I. *The Functions of the Executive.* Cambridge, Mass.: Harvard University Press, 1938.

4. Feller, Irwin, and others. *Sources and Uses of Scientific and Technological Information in State Legislatures.* University Park: Penn State University Institute for Research on Human Resources Center for the Study of Science Policy, 1975.

Additional Readings

Bowman, Joel P., and Branchaw, Bernadine P. *Successful Communication in Business.* San Francisco: Harper & Row, 1980. The latest of the basic skills texts encompassing topics from "Letters and Memos" to "Selling Yourself."

Kanter, Rosabeth. *Men and Women of the Corporation.* New York: Basic Books, 1978. This extensive case study of the administration of one organization examines how organizational constraints affect the meanings people make of their life and work. In particular, the constraints and rewards of managers, secretaries, and wives are explained using the concepts of "opportunity," "power," and "numbers."

Lawrence, Paul R., and Lorsch, Jay W. *Organization and Environment Managing Differentiation and Integration.* Cambridge, Mass.: Harvard University Press, 1968. In this major work on the "contingency approach" to understanding organizations, structure is shaped by environmental constraints. In effective organizations, different units evolve with different managerial styles and orientation to time constraints. These internal differences create problems communicating internally across department lines. An ongoing problem for potentially effective organizations is conflict resolution among departments.

Mintzberg, Henry. *The Nature of Managerial Work.* New York: Harper & Row, 1973. The research presented here is based on direct observations of five chief executives. Mintzberg found that managers work at an "unrelenting pace"; and they prefer oral to written communication. He outlines 10 working roles that executives must play: three interpersonal roles, three informational roles, and four decisional roles.

Pfeffer, Jeffrey, and Salancik, Gerald R. *The External Control of Organization.* New York: Harper & Row, 1978. Most management literature implies that the quality of administration has a major impact on organizational effectiveness. Research presented in this book argues the opposite: Administrative effect is dwarfed by environmental constraints. Communication and other strategies for manipulating the environment are described. The role of the executive is primarily symbolic.

Wildavsky, Aaron. *Speaking Truth to Power: The Art and Craft of Policy Analysis.* Boston: Little Brown, 1979. Ostensibly a guide for political scientists interested in public policy analysis, this book is actually a guide to the systematic use of political information in organizational decision making. For Wildavsky, "The highest form of analysis is using intellect to aid interaction between people."

CHAPTER 13

Pragmatic Communication

James F. Klumpp
Content Consultants: Thomas A. Hollihan
University of Southern California
David A. Thomas
Auburn University

The beginnings of decades are particularly appropriate times for charting where we have been and where we are going. This survey of pragmatic communication—"the study and practice of communication . . . to influence or facilitate decision making"[1]—focuses attention on the strategies necessary to cope with the dangers and opportunities that grow from the decade past. In society's decision-making institutions, the 60's and 70's were decades of social upheaval and cynicism, of Vietnam and Watergate. This mileau has produced a demand for a practical rhetoric that emphasizes personal effectiveness and institutional responsiveness in decision making. In education the past decade saw the final impact of the post-war baby boom and the economic strains of budget constraint. The result is a shifting student population and a new pragmatism in evaluating education. The future of pragmatic communication will be forged from these influences.

THE COMMUNITY AND THE CLASSROOM

Demands for practical education will bring the community and the classroom closer during the 80's. The back-to-basics movement's focus on the skills that prepare the educated to contribute to society,[2] the call for greater emphasis on lifelong learning,[3] and the growth of nontraditional forms of career education, such as vocational training and the two-year college, offer unusual opportunities for expanding the pragmatic communication curriculum in the 80's. Proponents of practical education value the skills of reasoning and effective expression, which are the center of argumentation, public speaking, and persuasion. Revitalized liberal arts concepts also stress the communicative skills. As a result the new practical students will find courses in pragmatic communication among the most attractive offered.

These curricular opportunities come as a consequence not only of the emphasis on careers but also of the dramatic social changes of the last two decades that have profoundly influenced the situations for public advocacy. A great paradox of that era was that even while cynicism spread and faith in institutions diminished,[4] the number of people actually involved in governmental decision making increased, especially at the local level. Citizens have become increasingly involved in community planning, neighborhood governing structures, and small claims courts. Born in the Vietnam protests, the environmental awakening, and the taxpayer revolts, citizen lobbies have created extensive new situations that require persons with communication skills. These activities suggest the need for courses taught in the community focusing on parliamentary procedure, strategies and tactics for influencing decision-making structures, and the communication skills with which to build successful citizen involvement organizations. Supplementing traditional courses in lobbying, debating, effective discussion, and persuasion, this curriculum opens public forums for greater participation.

Changes in classroom strategies should complement the expanded curriculum. The pragmatic communication classroom of the 80's should exploit the increasing awareness of communication in both business and government in order to provide opportunities for learning through involvement in the community. For example, a project that sends an architecture student into a neighborhood to sell her/his design for a neighborhood center will develop argumentative and persuasive skills in an atmosphere of excited involvement. Channeling a student's interest in a political candidate into a study of persuasion through participation in a campaign will intensify learning.

Of course, strategies such as these entail dangers. Most obviously, during a time when diminishing educational resources increase demands on teachers, the contact work and individual instruction necessary to implement such community involvement strategies multiply the burdens of time. In addition, exciting, but thin, courses too easily abandon firm grounding in established theory for glamorous projects that contribute less to understanding. In addition, efforts to develop relevant and situation-specific courses may lead the instructor too far afield into political strategy and legal elements in which expertise is limited. Simply, the disciplined teacher who is employing a community-oriented approach grounded in sound teaching strategies will find pragmatic communication a particularly advantageous perspective with which to encounter the social and educational changes of the 80's.

FORENSICS ACTIVITIES

No strategy for teaching pragmatic communication has as long a history of distinction as school forensics. Teachers of speech communication and their administrators should contemplate with care the marvels of forensics as an educational tool. It channels the ingrained American love for competition into an energetic investigation of decision making. It provides in the humanities and social sciences a laboratory for learning that has always been an advantage of the sciences and fine arts. The institutions developed for forensics competition—the tournaments, meets, or festivals—provide an intellectual community in the best sense of the word, where students have the benefit not only of close interaction with their instructor but also of the instructional resources of other schools. Is it any wonder that for generations this country's leaders have been molded by forensics?

As the 70's passed, forensics activities remained healthy, but the visible trends in society and education demand thoughtful strategies for an evolving conception of forensics in the 80's. The National Developmental Conference on Forensics (NDCF) provided an excellent, realistic review of the state of the forensics art. Many of the suggestions of that conference acquire new urgency in a new decade. For example, the new emphasis on personal involvement and responsiveness in public decision making provides greatly expanded opportunities for creative audience forensics activities on subjects of local interest.[5] Without intensive, preliminary skills preparation, the audience experience easily becomes mere exhibitionism; yet, the presence and reaction of the lay mind require communicability, a greater sense of feedback interaction, and persuasiveness—key skills in pragmatic communication. Such activities are also important resources to the community. Political debates have underlined the interest value generated by the competitive framework, and debate better illuminates the pro and con of issues than the strengths and weaknesses of political candidates. Other competitive forensics events also prepare students to knowledgeably inform the community on issues.

Forensics also must address the changing character of today's student. The narrow conceptualization of forensics encouraged by the visibility of the holistic tournament experience has contributed much to the image of forensics students as an intellectual elite fervently responding to demands for total commitment of time and effort. Today's student requires a program that recognizes a diversity of student goals, a limited commitment of time, and increasingly pragmatic concerns. Forensics educators may need to develop increased ability to teach isolated target skills through a diversity of activities.[6] For example, the "Protagoras" tournament format, which offers presorted evidence on a topic announced at the tournament, is a marvelous strategy for teaching argumentation, organization, and refutation, even though it may fail to teach the skills of research and advance preparation of subject matter. New events, such as the recent development of business skills meets, may also stimulate interest.

To totally abandon the present activity structure of forensics for these new strategies would be a serious error; yet, certainly the increasingly critical evaluation of educational programs demands realistic approaches to the future of competitive forensics. The most obvious danger is the financial crisis in education. School boards, caught between declining enrollments and taxpayer resistance, are forced to cut costs wherever possible. Colleges and universities face much the same fate as a result of the new governmental mood and the sagging economy. Upon surface examination, the staggering per-student cost of competitive forensics, when compared to that of classroom instruction, tags forensics as a convenient target for economy.[7] Meanwhile gasoline rationing and soaring energy costs continually threaten the continuation of transportation-intensive tournament forensics.

The pragmatic problems of educational finance create an even more serious problem—pressure on faculty. School boards faced with layoffs often consider speech communication to be a subject easily taught by English or drama instructors.[8] Colleges and universities demand more and more from their faculty for tenure and promotion, most often publication of research, and, in the process, they undervalue forensics.[9] As a result, forensics programs are often assigned to directors with nonacademic credentials, nonspeech backgrounds, or nonprofessorial ranks. Within forensics a tenuous dialectic has always existed between competition's natural inducement to gamesmanship and the educational goals induced most effectively by the academic conscience of professional forensics educators. Programs in which the director lacks credentials, background, or rank can too easily lose a healthy balance. The source of weakened cocurricular orientation is most often not the people involved but rather an institutional structure that ceases to provide the support and direction of the profession. Typical examples throughout the country indicate that even though forensics programs removed from the aegis of a full-time teacher of speech communication may remain temporarily competitive, they face diminished strength or even eventual elimination.

Few educational programs have shown more potential wisdom and foresight in meeting these pressures than has forensics. First, pragmatism in evaluation emphasizes results, and forensics educators must publicize and express pride in their success in training leaders. The pervasiveness of former forensics participants in positions of leadership in society demonstrates an influence that other programs under fire should envy.[10] Second, forensics must stress the centrality of excellence in the activity. To administrators facing declining enrollments, the rhetoric of excellence is increasingly important. To students facing larger and less demanding classes, excellence marks forensics as exceptional. Few activities are as attuned to excellence in goals, structure, and evaluation as forensics. Third, forensics educators must recognize that broad academic support for the activity best prepares a program for pragmatic evaluation. If forensics is to survive and grow, it must be an open community inviting feedback and suggestion, informing others of its goals and achievements, and opening its events to professional colleagues, administrators, and the public.[11] This may require educating the faculty and administrators on the aims of forensics and, frankly, even making some compromises in the conduct, objectives, and control of the forensics program. But forensics will not survive in educational systems organized as they are now without departmental and administrative support. Forensics programs provide departments and schools with positive publicity, an invaluable laboratory for cocurricular learning, and an attraction for the brightest students in the school. Departments and schools must provide the forensics program with the support needed in terms of time, money, and political pressure to help the programs and their directors advance.[12]

Few activities should be as well attuned to a more pragmatic decade as forensics. If forensics educators creatively address the changes in social and educational institutions, they will maintain the strength of present competitive forensics activities while adopting new outlets for forensics' demonstrated power to teach skills of leadership.

RESEARCH

As changes in society turn the attention of researchers to a wider variety of decision-making situations and as today's student demands a greater understanding of the pragmatic communication process, researchers seek to deepen their own understanding of how humans use language to negotiate and influence decisions. Consideration of the potential for meeting these opportunities must begin with the realization that no overall paradigm has united pragmatic communication research in the past. Argumentation research has focused largely on logic, recent forensics research on decision models, political communication research on media influences, and persuasion research on attitudes and psychosocial processes. Even these generalizations are questionable descriptions of fragmented studies. There is evidence of a paradigm emerging to organize research centers around several assumptions that spring from the nature of pragmatic communication:

1. *Humans choose.* Human beings face situations in their everyday experience that present alternative possibilities for interpretation and action, and in which humans have the power to choose.

2. *Human choice is social.* Each choice involves a sociocultural context, an effort to acquire social verification of choice, and a coordination of effort.

3. *The social choice process is symbolic.* Communication is the dialectic for negotiating interpretations and adapting action to situations and society.

Two images emerge from this set of assumptions: one holistic—society is developing institutions that facilitate sound choices in relatively stable patterns of cultural influence; and one contextual—humans are urging their choices upon others through communication. The approach to understanding the obvious complexity in these images will govern research. As the 70's closed, several lines of inquiry proceeded. One approach, for example, argues that rhetoric is epistemic, that pragmatic communication skills help us decide as symbol exchange orients us to a social knowledge and, thus, a decision.[13] Analyses of political and sociocultural decisions seek to reveal the ways in which the structure and style of language facilitate the decision-making process.[14] Other studies view argument as rule-governed, natural human behavior rather than as formal logic or as an institutional activity. The approach develops the rules, structure, and typology of reason-giving situations.[15]

Research may continue to be generally descriptive until an emerging paradigm clarifies the complexity. In addition, situational research that generalizes more narrowly—to political campaigns, to everyday conversational argument, to debates—will continue. Research methods will continue to range from historical to critical to theoretical to field research. We should expect pragmatic communication research to focus clearly on the human uses of communication. The interests of the field and the pragmatic needs of the moment encourage the generation of applicable knowledge on the impact of strategies—whether political communication research aimed at a more effective campaign strategy, conflict research aimed at more peaceful decision processes, or forensics research aimed at evaluating educational strategy.

CONCLUSION

Peering into the past and future transforms our conceptualization of the present. A moment of decision (which is, after all, the moment for which pragmatic communication should prepare us) becomes a seizing of the past's potential development to mold the future. Our past is not without its social and educational crises, but creative approaches to the 80's can prepare the pragmatic communication teacher for a fruitful decade. When the Chinese symbols for "opportunity" and "danger" are combined as a single symbol, it may be translated as "crisis." The crisis of the 70's presented us with a student population and a subject matter that creative teachers will mold into opportunity rather than danger.

REFERENCES

1. McBath, James H., and Jeffrey, Robert C. "Defining Speech Communication." *Communication Education* 27: 188; September 1978.

2. See especially: Hutchins, Robert M. "The Schools Must Stay." *The Center Magazine* 6: 12–23; January/February 1973. A particular application to pragmatic communication is the following: Phillips, Gerald M. "Rhetoric and the Proper Study of Man." *Communication Education* 27: 189–201; September 1978.

3. Hechinger, Fred M. "Education's 'New Majority.' " *Saturday Review* 20: 16; September 1975.

4. "Public Now Has Greater Confidence in Newspapers Than in Television." *Gallup Opinion Index* 166: 1–11; May 1979. This is the latest report on the erosion of institutional confidence. Although this cynicism is widely reported as a generic erosion, it should be emphasized that the decline is most dramatic with regard to the institutions of national government.

5. See: McBath, James H., editor. *Forensics as Communication.* Skokie, Ill.: National Textbook Co., 1975. pp. 15–16, 56.

6. *Ibid.*, pp. 29, 89, 97–98.

7. See: McBath, James H. "Beyond the Seventies." *Journal of the American Forensics Association* 8: 176; September 1972.

8. For a discussion of the dimensions and impact of this trend, see: McBath, James H., editor. *Forensics as Communication.* p. 144.

9. For a more detailed exploration of the dimensions of this problem, see: McBath, James H., editor. *Forensics as Communication.* pp. 47–48, 143–60.

10. The most recent of the volumes of evidence on this influence is the Bicentennial Youth Debates survey by Huseman and Goodman. They found that 78 percent of congressional respondents had participated in forensics. Of their respondents, 87 percent recognized the value of forensics in legislative work. Huseman, Richard C., and Goodman, Davis M. *Journal of the American Forensics Association* 12: 225–228; Spring 1976.

11. See especially: McBath, James H., editor. *Forensics as Communication.* pp. 85–88, 96.

12. The need for ties with speech communication was an important theme at the NDCF. See: McBath, James H., editor. *Forensics as Communication.* pp. 13–14, 47–49, 56–57, 85–88, 96–97.

13. For a review of the perspective see: Leff, Michael C. "In Search of Ariadne's Thread: A Review of the Recent Literature in Rhetorical Theory." *Central States Speech Journal* 29: 73–91; Summer 1978. The perspective is most clearly stated in: Cherwitz, Richard. "Rhetoric as a 'Way of Knowing': An Attenuation of the Epistemological Claims of the 'New Rhetoric.' " *Southern Speech Communication Journal* 42: 207–219; Spring 1977. The seminal works are: (1) Scott, Robert L. "On Viewing Rhetoric as Epistemic." *Central States Speech Journal* 18: 9–16; February 1967. (2) Scott, Robert L. "On Viewing Rhetoric as Epistemic: Ten Years Later." *Central States Speech Journal* 27: 258–266; Winter 1976.

14. Much of the work highlighting this approach to politics has been written by Murray Edelman. See, for example: Edelman, Murray. "The Language of Participation and the Language of Resistance." *Human Communication Research* 3: 159–170; Winter 1977. Works by speech communication scholars include: (1) Carpenter, Ronald H. "The Historical Jeremiad as Rhetorical Genre." *Form and Genre: Shaping Rhetorical Action.* (Edited by Karlyn Kohrs Campbell and Kathleen Hall Jamiesen.) Falls Church, Va.: Speech Communication Association, n.d. pp. 103–117. (2) Klumpp, James F., and Hollihan, Thomas A. "Debunking the Resignation of Earl Butz: Sacrificing an Official Racist." *Quarterly Journal of Speech* 65: 1–11; February 1979. (3) Bormann, Ernest G. "The Eagleton Affair: A Fantasy Theme Analysis." *Quarterly Journal of Speech* 59: 143–159; April 1973.

15. See: Willard, Charles A. "On the Utility of Descriptive Diagrams for the Analysis and Criticism of Arguments." *Communication Monographs* 43: 308–319; November 1976. Also: Willard, Charles A. "A Reformulation of the Concept of Argument: The Constructivist/ Interactionist Foundations of a Sociology of Argument." *Journal of the American Forensics Association* 14: 121–140; Winter 1978. See also: O'Keefe, Daniel J. "Two Concepts of Argument." *Journal of the American Forensics Association* 13: 121–128; Winter 1977. For research using the perspective see: (1) Jackson, Sally, and Jacobs, Scott. "Adjacency Pairs and the Sequential Description of Arguments." Paper presented at the Speech Communication Association convention, Minneapolis, 1978. (2) Willard, Charles A. "The Better Part of Valor: How Arguments 'Simmer Down' and Arguers Beat Retreats." Paper presented at the Speech Communication Association convention, San Antonio, 1979.

CHAPTER 14

Public Address

Bruce E. Gronbeck
Douglas M. Trank
Content Consultants: *Linda Moore*
University of Akron
Edward J. Pappas
Wayne State University

That which we term *public address* or *public speaking* or *public communication* represents an aggregate of skills that integrate and ultimately forward the interests of a culture. The prefix *com-* (from the Latin *cum* meaning "with") and *munus* (referring to a service performed for the society) are combined in our word *communication*—the idea of sharing experience publicly for the common good. We are concerned herein with the study of the efforts of some individuals, usually in communicative forms called *speeches* (but also in pamphlets, position papers, television commercials, etc.), to affect the beliefs, attitudes, values, and behaviors of the many in self-serving or socially beneficial manners.

Public address conjures up both positive and negative associations. Negatively, we often link the phrase with windy oratory, "mere" rhetoric, and knots in our stomachs when we rise "to say a few words" at city council meetings. More positively, we recreate visions of Winston Churchill's "blood sweat, and tears," John Kennedy's "New Frontier," and Martin Luther King, Jr.'s "dream." Public address, though abused by some, is a primary mode of communication for achieving social cohesion, social change, and common cultural purpose. It is operative not only on the grand ceremonial occasions, as when Presidents address Congress, the public, and the world via television, but also when people teach crafts at senior citizens' centers, offer opinions at school board meetings, engage in collective bargaining, and urge others to vote on the second Tuesday in November.

Public speaking, public communication, public address—these terms share a common referent; yet, they imply three rather different perspectives from which to examine public talk:

1. *Public speaking,* to most, connotes an interest in message building on the part of the individual, especially when that person must construct a "speech." From this perspective, one normally discusses *speakers, hearers, types of speeches, supporting materials, central ideas and theses, introductions and conclusions, organizational patterns, verbal and nonverbal delivery skills,* and the like. Those who talk about *public speaking* tend to view such phenomena as comprising a *personal act,* something one "does" in front of others.

2. *Public communication* is associated with investigations of the social–psychological–symbolic processes that enable one person to share beliefs, attitudes, values, and preferred actions with others. It is imbedded in a vocabulary—*sender* or *source, receiver, messages, channels, feedback, verbal and nonverbal symbols, psychological predispositions*—that reflects the *interactional or transactional aspects* of symbolic exchanges between persons. It is a perspective applicable not only to formal speeches but also to television commercials, radio call-in shows, exchanges in magazines, window displays, billboards, and so on. It tends to be more receiver-oriented than the public speaking perspective, at least comparatively.

3. *Public address* calls forth images of impassioned and eloquent orators formally exhorting a society during critical moments in the culture's history. One often discusses public address in terms of *speakers' roles* (politicians/clergy/agitators), *types* or *genres of talk* (inaugural addresses/sermons/conciliatory rhetoric), *styles of discourse* (17th-century style/British campaign oratory/Ciceronian forms), and *characterizations of collective audiences* (middle-class blacks/members of the National Rifle Association/Presbyterians). Those who analyze public address usually see speeches as *institutionalized rhetorical acts or transactions* between and among social units.

If these characterizations and vocabularies capture three distinct contexts from which to view public discoursing, then it follows that, educationally, we really have three sets of communication-related skills. The sets of skills are interrelated because they all comprehend "public talk"; yet, they are discrete in that they emphasize relatively distinct aspects of speaking. We may term these sets *message-generating, message-consumption, and message-analysis skills:* Teachers of public speaking tend to focus on techniques for constructing messages, teachers of public communication on ways we react to messages from different channels, and teachers of public address on methods for analyzing and evaluating speeches and their effects upon society. Ideally, of course, a speech communication teacher should be working on all three sets of skills. But let us examine one set at a time.

MESSAGE-GENERATING SKILLS

The art of teaching people how to construct speeches, we assume, has been practiced at least since the 5th century B.C., when two rhetoricians (Corax and Tisias of Syracuse) prepared handbooks to help landowning clients reclaim familial property following a major revolution in the Greek city states. Concern for skills in public speaking has remained unabated through the centuries, and even today, survey after survey reveals that people want educational curriculums that include training in speechmaking. We can conveniently group such skills under three heads:

Preperformance Skills

1. Selecting a general purpose (to inform, persuade, inspire, move to action)
2. Phrasing a specific purpose (to tell audience x about y, etc.)
3. Analyzing the audience's demographic characteristics (age, sex, group memberships, ethnic background) and internal beliefs, attitudes, and values relative to a topic, so as to better adapt the speech to them
4. Searching for material relevant to the speech's purpose, thesis, or central idea and its audience
5. Organizing the material into a coherent pattern
6. Preparing both an introduction that heightens the speaker's credibility, gains attention, and orients the audience, and a conclusion that summarizes the material and offers additional inducement
7. Wording key concepts in the speech purposively and effectively

8. Practicing the speech to gain confidence and oral–behavioral control over the material.

Performance Skills

1. Delivering the speech in an oral style (linguistic skills)
2. Taking care that pronunciation, loudness, rate, and vocal variety reinforce the meaning of ideas and the emotional atmosphere sought (paralinguistic skills)
3. Standing and moving so as to communicate accurately the speaker's attitudes toward self, the topic, and others (proxemic skills)
4. Using appropriate facial expressions and gestures (kinesic skills)
5. Employing visual aids when appropriate (visualizing skills).

Postperformance Skills

1. Examining one's own reactions to speaking after having done it (self-evaluation)
2. Diagnosing the feedback to one's performance (others-evaluation).

These three lists include only the most general message-generating skills. Each, in turn, can be cast into specific instructional objectives. So, for example, performance skill 2 can be subdivided, with the aid of taxonomies of objectives,[1] into skills in the *cognitive domain* (e.g., distinguishing between *formal* and *informal* pronunciation patterns), the *affective domain* (e.g., reporting personal preferences for formal or informal patterns), and the *psychomotor domain* (e.g., recreating vocally the formal and informal patterns).

MESSAGE-CONSUMPTION SKILLS

Ever since Isocrates wrote *Against the Sophists* (c. 390 B.C.), teachers of speech communication have agonized over the effects and ethics of public talk. The same is true today. Shortly after the words *communication* and *process* came into vogue following World War II, "listening" experts sprang up. Some scholars—e.g., Ralph Nichols and Leonard Stevens— were concerned primarily with accurate listening, but soon writers such as Marshall McLuhan *(The Mechanical Bride)* and Vance Packard *(The Hidden Persuaders)* were preaching the gospel of defensive or critical listening. All soon agreed that listening is not a passive activity; message consumption involves not only comprehension (receiving and attending to a message) but also interpretation (assigning meaning to a message) and evaluation (reacting to a message). We, therefore, ought to be teaching three sets of listening skills.

Comprehension Skills

1. Understanding the central idea or thesis of a message
2. Identifying the ideas, arguments, and materials that support the assertions
3. Enumerating the main segments of a message, along with the various linguistic and nonverbal signposts that indicate intellectual movement, change, or interrelationships among ideas.

Interpretation Skills

1. Forming an image of the source's "self" (trustworthy/dynamic/competent/involved/detached)
2. Detecting the message's emotional thrust (urgent/fearful/entertaining/ironic/paradoxical)
3. Specifying the suitability of the message to the channels (face-to-face/print/electronic/iconic), the occasion, the subject matter, and the receivers.

Evaluation Skills

1. Testing the adequacy of the proof or support offered for assertions
2. Checking the reasoning for formal and informal fallacies
3. Assessing the source's intents and ethical posture
4. Deciding how much of the message to accept or reject.

These are only the most general skills categories, and, of course, these domains, too, can be subdivided with the help of more specific instructional objectives.[2] And we believe that students must exercise these skills in the consumption of not only oral messages but also print and nonprint messages (ads, billboards, newspapers, TV, radio, and the like).

MESSAGE-ANALYSIS SKILLS

From critical listening it is but a short step to more formal analyses of the worlds of politics, religion, social agitation, self-help movements, investigative reporting, judicial proceedings, and international sabre rattling. Because *public address* remains vital in times of war and peace, it deserves systematic examination by students.

Whether one is attempting to measure the effects of oratory, to explore the uses of ideological language by demagogues, to classify speeches and broadcasts into genres so as to understand tradition and ceremony in public address, or to plumb the core of social identity to be found in great speeches, one always needs particular skills to be an effective historian or critic.

Research Skills

1. Finding accurate texts of speeches and video- or audiotapes of other artifacts

2. Using newspaper accounts, biographies, and memoirs; votes recorded in official proceedings; public opinion polls; etc., to assess the effects of public messages

3. Conducting interviews and surveys to investigate systematically reactions to messages

4. Dissecting model critical essays to discover ways of recording one's ideas and reactions.

Analytical Skills

1. Determining speakers' purposes, attitudes toward the audience/situation/topic, ethical constraints, and self-conceptions

2. Classifying arguments, metaphors, valuative appeals, and so forth in systematic ways

3. Finding ways to relate what is discovered within the message to any psychological or sociological models available in order to account for effects, cultural significations, institutional changes, and the like that one is interested in.

Writing Skills

1. Understanding the purposes or functions of historical and critical writing

2. Translating one's own writing purposes into established formats or models for historical and critical essays

3. Discovering evidence for one's critical claims

4. Gaining a sense of the vocabulary, essay structures, footnote forms, and the like that are habitually used in historical and critical writing

5. Finding one's "voice" in essays and research papers.

Obviously, we here are treating relatively sophisticated skills. Yet, the notion that students of all ages should be taught, specifically and systematically, to deal with *public address,* which ultimately governs their lives and environment, must be underscored. To ignore public talk is to leave students uninformed and unarmed.

PUBLIC ADDRESS IN THE 80'S

Thanks to Title II of the 1978 Elementary and Secondary Education Act and the growing sensitivity to the need for adequate language arts education at all levels, the sets of skills we have reviewed herein are now being recognized as crucial. Students must learn not only how to read and write but also how to talk, listen, and analyze effectively. As we upgrade teacher preparation—through more rigorous certification requirements, summer institutes and workshops, and in-service training sessions—the study of public address will achieve renewed sophistication in the 80's:

1. Language Arts Resource Specialists (LARS personnel) will develop programs for oral as well as written language training in both elementary and secondary educational institutions.

2. Listening, particularly, will receive primary emphasis at all levels of education.

3. While training in speechmaking will occur primarily in secondary and college educational institutions, rudimentary message generation will be featured in elementary programs. "Show and tell" will be replaced with oral report assignments in elementary social studies, science, music, and literature units.

4. With the increasing availability of videotape resources, message-analysis training will expand. As a growing number of prepackaged television viewing services is available to secondary teachers, especially, television specials and regular pro-

grams should provide materials to use in teaching students to criticize and evaluate rhetorical messages.

The ability to talk—to use symbols purposively—has been vital to the emergence of our planet's various cultures. Education in the 80's will have to reflect a determination to prepare the young for lives of public self-fulfillment and service.

REFERENCES

1. See: (1) Bloom, Benjamin S., and others. *Taxonomy of Educational Objectives—The Classification of Educational Goals, Handbook I: Cognitive Domain.* New York: David McKay Co., 1956. (2) Krathwohl, David R., and others. *Taxonomy of Educational Objectives—The Classification of Educational Goals, Handbook II: Affective Domain.* New York: David McKay Co., 1964. (3) Kibler, Robert J., and others. *Behavioral Objectives and Instruction.* Boston: Allyn and Bacon, 1970. The first two books survey objectives in the cognitive and affective domains; because the committee putting them out has yet to complete the third volume (psychomotor domain), instructors should go to *Behavioral Objectives and Instruction* to complete the trio.

2. Wolvin, Andrew R., and Coakley, Carolyn Gwynn. *Listening Instruction.* Urbana, Ill.: ERIC/RCS, 1979. [Also available from the Speech Communication Association, 5105 Backlick Road, Annandale, Va. 22003, as part of the SCA's TRIP (Theory and Research Into Practice) series.] A booklet designed to aid high school and college instructors in designing and teaching units or courses in five types of listening—appreciative, discriminative, comprehensive, therapeutic, and critical. Includes 38 exercises with objectives, instructions, discussion questions, and bibliography.

CHAPTER 15

Rhetorical Theory: Indications for the Future

Karlyn Kohrs Campbell
Kathleen M. Hall Jamieson
Content Consultants: Trevor Melia
University of Pittsburgh
Robert L. Scott
University of Minnesota

Students of rhetoric examine the art of using symbols; more particularly, they look at how, why, and to what effect persons use and create symbols. They study language as addressed to others, as adapted to be intelligible and appealing, and as structured to justify ends and means in terms of cultural values. In contrast to the sciences and philosophy, which strive to create abstract statements that will apply regardless of particular persons in particular circumstances, the concern of rhetoric is with social truths that are created and validated by people. Thus, students of rhetoric must consider all of the means by which symbols are used to create social truths.

As a field of study or an area of expertise, rhetoric presumes that symbolic acts can be scrutinized usefully as distinct phenomena. As a discipline, rhetoric is the record of past efforts to understand symbols, and it generates theories explaining symbolic acts, a lexicon of terms for central concepts and processes, and experimentation and criticism to test and to refine theory and practice.

A theory embodies the knowledge gathered and systematically structured by experienced observers in terms of interrelated assumptions or principles so that it can be used to analyze and/or explain a distinct set of phenomena. A fully developed rhetorical theory capable of accounting for relevant symbolic action must include the following: (1) a human ontology explaining how and why people are capable of and subject to persuasion, (2) an epistemology describing the role of symbols in the processes by which truths are created and/or discovered, and (3) an axiology indicating the standards by which rhetorical acts can be judged. These elements are essential because rhetorical theory must explain how influence is possible, define the relationship between symbolic and nonsymbolic reality, and delineate principles for understanding and evaluating the role of symbolic acts in social decision making. Theorizing has emphasized human ontology, with particular concern for the rhetorical potential implicit in the rational capacities and psycho-physiological needs of humans.

Contemporary scholarship has focused its attention on unearthing the presuppositions underlying major perspectives on rhetoric. The dominant theory, derived from Aristotle, has been extensively analyzed and criticized. The theories derived from the various psychological schools have also been described and analyzed. In addition, some rhetorical theorists have posited alternative perspectives, frequently generated as a result of the ideas found in works of modern philosophers and literary scholars. That rhetorical theory is in a period of transition is signalled by the close scrutiny of existing theories and by attempts to generate new perspectives. Major developments that may be expected to influence rhetorical theory in the 1980's are indicated below.

In contrast to earlier periods in which theory emphasized the rhetor, the audience, and the occasion as discrete, co-equal categories, contemporary theory focuses on the symbolic act. This shift is evidenced by an increasing interest in rhetorical criticism and by the development of discourse analysis, speech act theory, and ethnographic methodology. It is also reflected in the growing importance of dramatistic and phenomenological approaches to rhetoric and of constructivistic approaches to the study of symbolic acts. Since dramatism treats language as a mode of action rather than as a means of transmitting information, and since phenomenology emphasizes the role of human symbolizing in the construction of reality, they are particularly suited to theorizing that focuses on messages. Dramatistic studies presume the integrated character of the act, the actor, the context, the symbolic medium, and the function of the act. Phenomenology presumes interrelationships among the actor, the act, the symbol, and nonsymbolic reality. Thus, both have received increasing attention because they recognize the complexity of symbolic action.

In an attempt to define an epistemology appropriate to rhetoric, contemporary rhetorical theorists have explored the rhetorical character of social knowledge. This development has been buttressed by recent scientific data corroborating the contingent character of all knowledge and the impact of the observer on what is observed. Theory has also probed the relationships between ideology or world view and concepts of knowledge, and among the character of the agent or source and the meaning of a message and the claims that it makes. Special efforts have been made to define the nature of argument and the conditions under which it can occur, and to ascertain the degree to which arguments are field-dependent or vary according to function. Generally, rhetoric based on a priori concepts of truth has been compared and contrasted to rhetoric based on concepts of knowledge as socially constructed or created.

Whereas past theory was pre-eminently meant to explain individual symbolic acts, the concern of contemporary theory has shifted toward the study of movements, campaigns, and genres. This shift reflects a recognition of the complexity of symbolic action and a desire to develop theory accounting for patterns of discourse that persist over time and for conventions, established by prior rhetoric, that influence subsequent rhetorical action. In developing a theory of movements, campaigns, and genres, contemporary theorists have explored the interrelationships among issues, lines of argument, stylistic conventions, and situations that shape and constrain symbolic strategies. Studies of movements and genres have probed recurrent forms and broadened comprehension of the kinds of purposes of symbolic action. They have also impelled efforts to understand such nondiscursive symbolic forms as confrontative rhetorical acts and such apparently self-defeating acts as the diatribe.

The work of intellectual historians such as Walter Ong has spurred theorists to consider how concepts of rhetoric are altered by time and culture, and how the nature of symbolic action and its functions are transformed by shifts in the dominant medium of communication. Closely related to such efforts is a recognition that what has been called rhetorical theory is Western, Greco-Roman theory, and that this theory needs to be supplemented and refined by non-Western perspectives such as those emanating from Arabic, Oriental, and American Indian cultures, among others.

Efforts have been made to clarify, extend, and modify the rhetorical lexicon. Yet the canon of style, particularly metaphor, requires additional study to define the character and assess the impact of aesthetic, nondiscursive, nonpropositional rhetorical strategies. Despite efforts to study the nature of meaning, further study of metacommunication—

i.e., framing, double binds, and so forth—is needed. The canon of disposition has received only sporadic contemporary analysis, and our understanding of structure remains rudimentary. The concepts of "the people" and of "the universal audience" have refined the traditional notion of the audience as passive to include the notion of the audience both as a potential agent of change that, indeed, may be created by the discourse, and as a shifting entity that alters over time and is subdivided differently by public discourses.

The synthetic theorizing of Northrop Frye, Kenneth Burke, and Ernst Cassirer suggests that an encompassing and unifying rhetorical theory can be developed to account for highly disparate symbolic acts. Such theory also suggests the continuing importance of the concepts of form, archetype, and myth in scholarship on the human use of symbols.

It is probable that an increasing number of messages in the 1980's will emanate from impersonal and institutional sources, and such messages will force refinement or alteration of the concepts of character and credibility. More and more messages will be transmitted by mass media and shaped by technological advances such as two-way cable, videophones, and the like. Communication in the classroom will be transformed. Two-way communication between distant locations can link a class in New York to a class in Tucson, or connect a Spanish-speaking teacher to Hispanic children throughout a school system. Theory will have to be developed to account for these phenomena as well as for ostensibly "personal" computer-created messages selectively addressed to mass audiences. Such theory will have to account for personalized direct mail advertising and also for student-tailored interactional computer programs that will be used to teach such basic skills as reading and mathematics and to facilitate recall in such courses as history and geography.

In addition, those who will be developing future rhetorical theory must consider the changing qualities of the dominant mass medium—television—and must account for its special rhetorical use of visual symbols, the definition of time that it enforces, and the rhetorical conventions it imposes on both televised and nontelevised messages. For example, television creates expectations in audiences that messages will be simple rather than complex, that they will be of a predictable length, and that they will be filled with dramatic but resolvable conflicts. Finally, rhetorical theorists will need to examine how public messages, transmitted and shaped by the mass media, influence the symbolic acts within families and communities.

Additional Readings

Bryant, Donald. "Rhetoric: Its Functions and Its Scope." *Quarterly Journal of Speech* 39: 401–424; December 1953. A clear and cogent essay on the nature of rhetoric which serves as an excellent starting point in exploring theory. For more recent comments on this essay, see also: Bryant, Donald. *Rhetorical Dimensions in Criticism.* Baton Rouge: Louisana State University Press, 1973. pp. 3–23.

Burke, Kenneth. "Definition of Man." *Language as Symbolic Action.* Berkeley: University of California Press, 1966. pp. 3–24. A challenging and provocative essay on the central role of symbolicity in human ontology.

Campbell, Karlyn Kohrs. "The Ontological Foundations of Rhetorical Theory." *Philosophy & Rhetoric* 3: 97–108; Spring 1970. This essay explores three major views of human ontology and describes the sorts of rhetorical theory each entails.

Delia, Jesse G. "Constructivism and the Study of Human Communication." *Quarterly Journal of Speech* 63: 66–83; February 1977. This essay specifies the basic assumptions underlying an approach to communication that views as central the role of the individual in interpreting messages.

Farrell, Thomas B. "Knowledge, Consensus, and Rhetorical Theory." *Quarterly Journal of Speech* 62: 1–14; February 1976. Also: Carleton, Walter M. "What Is Rhetorical Knowledge: A Response to Farrell—and More." And: Farrell, Thomas B. "Social Knowledge II." *Quarterly Journal of Speech* 64: 313–334; October 1978. This set of essays is a dialogue about the nature of the relationship between rhetoric and social knowledge.

Hawes, Leonard C. "Elements of a Model for Communication Process." *Quarterly Journal of Speech* 59: 11–21; February 1973. This essay attempts to describe and develop a model for communication that takes account of the fact that it is a process.

McGee, Michael C. "In Search of 'The People': A Rhetorical Alternative." *Quarterly Journal of Speech* 61: 235–249; October 1975. This essay surveys past conceptions of the audience and suggests a new conception related to culture, ideology, and historical period.

Murphy, James J. "The Four Ancient Traditions." *Rhetoric in the Middle Ages: A History of Rhetorical Theory from St. Augustine to the Renaissance.* Berkeley: University of California Press, 1974. pp. 3–42. This is an excellent introduction to the historical sources of varied perspectives on rhetoric and rhetorical theory.

Ong, Walter J. *Interfaces of the Word: Studies in the Evolution of Consciousness and Culture.* Ithaca, N.Y.: Cornell University Press, 1977. This collection of essays is a history of the evolution of consciousness and culture as influenced by the media of communication and an argument that all communicative systems are interrelated, affecting one another.

CHAPTER 16

Implications of Oral Communication As a Basic Skill

Carolyn M. Del Polito
Barbara Lieb-Brilhart
Content Consultants: Kenneth L. Brown
University of Massachusetts
Cassandra L. Book
Michigan State University

During the early years of American education, the ability to speak articulately and persuasively was viewed as a *basic* part of one's education. Eighteenth century classrooms were dominated by speech activities including lectures, recitations, declamations, debates, and dramatic dialogues. During the nineteenth century, discussion and conversation surfaced, precursors to the broader and more functional speech activities appearing in modern curriculums. Teachers understood that skills in selecting, organizing, and presenting ideas to influence an audience had to be learned just as systematically as the skills of reading and writing.

Unfortunately, the view of oral communication as basic to each student's education declined during the first half of the twentieth century; its status became primarily that of an elective or an extracurricular activity in the English curriculum. The rise of silent reading in the nineteenth century and an emphasis on literature and composition contributed to the twentieth century educators' perceptions of the "speech arts" as curricular frills.

Notably, at the same time when many English teachers and other educators were de-emphasizing oral communication, a small group of educators continued to study and teach speech communication and to foster a separate and expanding discipline. During the 1950's, speech researchers and educators began to emphasize the interactive nature of the speaking and listening processes. As more was learned about the complexities of communication, enthusiasm lessened for speech as a behavior to be rehearsed for the acquisition of trophies. Researchers and educators focused on the receiver in the process of communication, and oral communication instruction began to emphasize speaking and listening as everyday communicative acts. The study of nonverbal communication (e.g., facial expression, use of space, vocal cues, etc.) by social scientists also added new dimensions to oral communication instruction. Recent curriculums also reflect the belief that people need to develop their speaking and listening abilities for many situations: for example, one-to-one contexts (conversing, counseling, interviewing, etc.), small-group contexts (for accomplishing tasks, problem solving, etc.), one-to-large-group or public communication contexts, and mediated contexts (where critical listening and viewing behaviors become increasingly important).

Even today, however, there are two conflicting trends that affect our profession. On the one hand, there is a reluctance to accept the notion that oral communication instruction is necessary for all students and that resources need to be provided to implement programs. On the other hand, there is growing support for oral communication as a critical part of one's *basic* education.

Supporting the first trend is the reality of current school programs. While most educators acknowledge the importance of such education, most students with "normal" speech development receive little formal training in speech communication after age six. Because children enter school using the oral code (unlike their use of the written code), the myth persists that further education in the skills of speaking and listening is unnecessary. Recent data from the National Center for Educational Statistics indicate that, at best, only 65 percent of senior high schools offer identifiable speech communication courses. Of these schools, very few require speech courses for graduation. Speaking and listening skills still are taught predominantly in the context of English electives, mainly for the "elite" who already perform well in oral communication activities. At the elementary level, such instruction is either fortuitous, contingent upon the teacher's training and interests, or targeted for students with communication disorders in the context of special education.

This dismal picture is counterbalanced by the growing awareness that oral communication is central to an individual's academic, career, and personal success. Research evidence increasingly points to the centrality of oral communication competencies in the development of reading and writing skills, as well as in achievement in other areas of the curriculum. Numerous studies also support the need for such skills as effective speaking and conference leadership among top and middle management personnel. In addition to courses in public speaking, which have long been part of many industries' educational programs, there is an increasing emphasis on listening instruction to prevent communication breakdowns.

In response to these needs and in recognition of the importance of oral communication in educational programs, some state education agencies are beginning to revise their definitions of literacy to include abilities in oral communication. More importantly, in 1978, Congress revised the National Reading Act and passed the Basic Skills Proficiency Act (Elementary and Secondary Education Act, Title II), expanding the view of basic skills to include reading, mathematics, and effective communication, both written and *oral.* As speech communication educators, we applaud the wisdom of our legislators, but we also recognize the increased demands placed on us to provide curricular resources, staff development programs, and assessment models in oral communication for state and local education agencies.

The reaffirmation of oral communication as a basic skill in the education of all pupils in the 1980's presents challenges not faced by our eighteenth century counterparts. Specifically, the teacher of speech communication will be challenged by three influences: (1) a holistic movement in instruction; (2) accelerating societal complexities and technological advances; and (3) changing learning environments.

ESEA Title II legislation and regulations purposely did not define the basic skills beyond the broad categories of reading, mathematics, and effective communication, both written and oral—leaving specific definitions to the professional communities and to the national organizations. These agencies, in turn, are assisting teachers, administrators, and officials of state departments of education in designing effective programs which integrate basic skills with the content areas. Importantly, the national organizations representing each of the basic skills disciplines have rejected the "minimal" notion of "basics," as evidenced by the dearth of materials prepared for their members in response to the ESEA Title II legislation.

For oral communication, the Speech Communication Association (SCA), along with the American Speech–Language–Hearing Association (ASHA), has developed *Standards for Effective Oral Communication Programs*[1] as guidelines for teachers and administrators who are developing and/or evaluating their programs. Within these *Standards,* the definition of oral communication reflects the current emphasis in communication education. Thus, oral communication is defined as the process of interacting through heard and spoken messages in a variety of situations. Effective oral communication is a learned behavior, involving the following processes:

1. *Speaking in a variety of educational and social situations.* Speaking involves, but is not limited to, arranging and producing messages through the use of voice, articulation, vocabulary, syntax, and nonverbal cues (e.g., gesture, facial expression, vocal cues) appropriate to the speaker and listeners.

2. *Listening in a variety of educational and social situations.* Listening involves, but is not limited to, hearing, perceiving, discriminating, interpreting, synthesizing, evaluating, organizing, and remembering information from verbal and nonverbal messages.

While the *Standards* emphasize systemic instruction in oral communication in a well-defined portion of the curriculum, they also stress *integration* of communication competencies with other academic areas. This integrated, holistic approach has been reinforced in a recent document, the *Essentials of Education,* developed and supported by a large number of educational and administrative organizations (including SCA). As stated in the *Essentials* document:

> The interdependence of skills and content is the central concept of the essentials of education. Skills and abilities do not grow in isolation from content. In all subjects, students develop skills in using language and other symbol systems; they develop the ability to reason; they undergo experiences that lead to emotional and social maturity. Students master these skills and abilities through observing, listening, reading, talking, and writing *about* science, mathematics, history and the social sciences, the arts and other aspects of our intellectual, social and cultural heritage. As they learn about their world and its heritage they necessarily deepen their skills in language and reasoning and acquire the basis for emotional, aesthetic and social growth.[2]

As teachers of the 1980's and the 1990's, we will be challenged to become more creative, not only in integrating skills with content areas but also in adapting to accelerating *societal complexities* and *technological advances.* While we may be amazed by the current low-cost portable computers, calculators, and microprocessors, in 10 years educational technology (including noncomputer linked, home-based television programming and sophisticated computor-assisted instruction) will be "three times as productive at one-half the cost."[3]

Thus, we must be not only especially competent communicators and teachers of speech communication but also consultants to all teachers in utilizing the basic skills in all content areas. For example, we must begin preparing ourselves, our colleagues, and our students to cope with the rapid technological advances and possible elimination (or at least limitation) of interpersonal contact. Perhaps more challenging is the threat of increased propaganda disguised as educational programming.

The new decade may reveal that our definitions of communication competence are inaccurate, or at least that they require revision. Perhaps, as Christopher J. Dede suggests, new types of communication skills will be needed when using a machine as an intermediary:

> . . . we may see innovative communications styles that will allow us to be person oriented and effective even when sending messages via the computer or television.[4]

Along with low-cost and innovative instructional technology, current population and immigration statistics indicate *rapidly shifting populations* among student groups. We can expect large increases in non-English-speaking and mainstreamed students at both the elementary and the secondary levels. In addition, the emphasis on life-long learning will require instructional communication behaviors adaptable to a variety of learners.

This is our challenge for the 80's. As speech communication professionals, we need to recognize our new roles and responsibilities, and to mobilize our efforts at both the elementary and the secondary levels.

At the elementary level, in addition to those teachers who identify and remediate communication disorders, we must have specialists who can assist basic skills and content teachers in strengthening their students' communication skills by developing and demonstrating appropriate instruction and assessment procedures; assist colleagues in solving communication problems, particularly in multicultural and mainstreamed special education classrooms; and assist teachers, parents, and administrators in recognizing the importance of oral communication instruction to the child's further social and academic development.

At the secondary level, the demands for basic instruction and integration will be even greater. The Youth Employment and Demonstration Act focuses on support for the basic education of disadvantaged high school students. Along with the disadvantaged, the gifted and the handicapped will require specialized classroom communication strategies. Harold G. Shane, in *Curriculum Change Toward the 21st Century,* emphasized the priority for all students to be able to use "language without ambiguity and with an understanding of the ways in which messages influence the attitudes and mediate the behaviors of others."[5]

To be prepared for changing enrollments, increased technology, and instructional staff needs, speech communication specialists at the secondary level must do the following: (1) assist colleagues in other disciplines in understanding communication concepts and in integrating effective communication strategies into classroom instruction; (2) assist colleagues and students in coping with a changing technological society, and ensure effective communication experiences for all; and (3) develop and implement speech communication, theatre, and mass communication programs in educational and community settings.

These new roles will require new perceptions of ourselves as teachers, including the recognition of ourselves as consultants/resource persons, participant researchers, child advocates, and active professionals, interacting not only with individuals in our local school and community but also with local and state government and education leaders. As experts in oral communication, we will be called upon for our recommendations regarding a myriad of communication-related activities—and we need to be prepared.

There are a variety of resources that will help prepare speech communication professionals for their new roles and responsibilities in the 1980's and help meet the demands of local, state, and federal initiatives in basic skills. Along with graduate courses in communication, continuing education and professional development can accrue through active participation in national, regional, and state associations.

Currently, the Speech Communication Association (SCA), the national organization for teachers of speech communication, is directing major attention to communication skills development and assessment. In cooperation with other organizations, SCA has sponsored a number of projects and developed a variety of resource materials related to oral communication competence, including approaches to teaching oral communication at all levels; standards for effective oral communication programs at the elementary and secondary levels, and criteria for evaluating instruments that assess oral communication competence.

SCA is also disseminating a Resource Packet, entitled *Resources for Assessment in Communication,* [6] which includes a listing of consultants in communication and a selected annotated bibliography on *Assessment of Basic Oral Communication Skills.* The SCA also sponsors conferences, short courses, journals, newsletters, and numerous publications to assist professionals concerned with oral communication.

In addition to the Speech Communication Association, there are other professional communication organizations that provide relevant educational and professional growth opportunities through their journals, newsletters, and annual meetings. For example, most states have speech communication associations, and each of the four regions (Eastern, Southern, Central, and Western) has its own communication association to help meet members' needs. (For details regarding your regional and state communication associations, contact the Speech Communication Association, 5101 Backlick Road, Annandale, Va. 22003.)

To enhance the oral communication abilities of our children and youth, and to promote oral communication as basic to their future careers and social success, speech communication professionals of the 1980's will need to acquire new roles, new self-perceptions, new knowledge, and new access to resources. The future of oral communication as a basic skill will depend upon our effectiveness as speech communication professionals to vocally support our discipline in our schools and in our legislatures; our ability as speech communication researchers to provide answers to the many communication skills questions posed by teachers, parents, and administrators alike; and our willingness to adapt an old and well-respected discipline to the needs of learners living in a complex and rapidly changing society.

REFERENCES

1. *The Standards for Effective Oral Communication Programs* (1978), prepared by the Speech Communication Association and the American Speech–Language–Hearing Association, is available in brochure form from the Speech Communication Association, 5105 Backlick Road, Annandale, Va. 22003 (single copies free).

2. The document prepared by the organizations for the *Essentials of Education* (1979) is available in brochure form from the Speech Communication Association, 5105 Backlick Road, Annandale, Va. 22003 (single copies free).

3. Dede, Christopher J. "Educational Technology: The Next Ten Years." Paper presented at the Chief State School Officers' Summer Institute, July 1979. p. 8.

4. *Ibid.*, p. 14.

5. Shane, Harold G. *Curriculum Change Toward the 21st Century.* Washington, D.C.: National Education Association, 1977. p. 65.

6. For a copy of *Resources for Assessment in Communication* (1980), contact the Speech Communication Association, 5105 Backlick Road, Annandale, Va. 22003 (single copies $1.00 prepaid).

Additional Readings

Allen, R.R., and Brown, Kenneth L., editors. *Developing Communication Competence in Children.* Skokie, Ill.: National Textbook Co., 1979. An excellent review of literature on the cognitive, social, and communication development of children. Provides a synthesis of data that examines the definition of communication competence and specifies implications for research and instruction.

Basic Skills Synthesis Project Report. Available from Spencer Ward, The National Institute of Education, 1200 19th St., N.W., Washington, D.C. A review and synthesis of current issues and instructional choices for each of the basic skills: reading, writing, mathematics, and oral communication.

Brown, Kenneth, and others. *Assessment of Basic Speaking and Listening Skills: State of the Art and Recommendations for Instrument Development.* CS 502 686. Boston: Massachusetts State Department of Education, 1979. Volumes I and II.

Larson, C., and others. *Assessing Functional Communication.* ED 153 275. Falls Church, Va.: Speech Communication Association, 1978. Identifies and describes conceptual and methodological issues involved in evaluating the major components of interpersonal interaction related to functional communication. Part II contains brief reviews of 90 instruments designed to generate information on some aspect of functional communication.

"Redefining Literacy: Speaking and Listening as Basics." *Communication Education,* Volume 27, November 1978. This issue addresses a number of questions related to oral communication as a basic skill, including defining literacy, teaching functional communication skills at both the elementary and the secondary levels, assessing communication competencies, and needed research.

Additional resources are available from the Speech Communication Association, 5105 Backlick Road, Annandale, Va. 22003, and the ERIC/RCS Module at the SCA office.

CHAPTER 17

Special Needs of Handicapped, Reticent, Gifted, Bilingual, and Female Students

Paul G. Friedman
Content Consultants: David E. Butt
Pennsylvania State University
Theodore G. Groves
Portland State University

INTRODUCTION

The civil rights movement of the 1960's and 1970's had dramatic effects on every primary social institution, including the public schools. Rights previously ignored or denied, for a wide range of groups, are now recognized and protected by law. The legal mandate to provide an equal, appropriate education for all students has presented educators with unprecedented challenges. The 1980's is a decade during which schools must devote attention and resources to meet the needs of *all* students, especially those previously neglected. This chapter will discuss how teachers in grades K–12 who are especially concerned with the speech communication process can accommodate the newly identified needs of handicapped, reticent, gifted, bilingual, and female students in their classes.

HANDICAPPED STUDENTS

The Education for All Handicapped Children Act (PL 94-142), enacted on November 29, 1975, requires that all handicapped children be appropriately educated in the least restrictive environment possible.

Handicapped children are defined in Section 121a.5 of the regulations as those evaluated—

> as being mentally retarded, hard of hearing, deaf, speech impaired, visually handicapped, seriously emotionally disturbed, orthopedically impaired, other health impaired, deaf-blind, multi-handicapped, or as having specific learning disabilities, who because of those impairments need special education and related services.

The passage of PL 94-142 has led to the widespread adoption of a process called *mainstreaming*—educating handicapped children in regular classrooms to the maximum extent appropriate for each child. Mainstreaming was justified by studies that revealed negative effects from labeling and segregating the handicapped in special classes and that found, for the most part, that handicapped students do better academically in regular classes. Mainstreaming expresses the desire to focus on the strengths and learning potential of students, in contrast to the historical preoccupation in special services with their deficits. The law provides for placement procedures, independent review, due process, written individualized education plans (IEPs), and a host of other procedural safeguards for these children.

The classroom teacher first becomes actively involved with mainstreaming when an IEP is developed. That occurs at a meeting which, by law, must be held at least once a year and must include, besides the regular teacher, a special education teacher, one or both of the child's parents, the child (where appropriate), and other individuals at the discretion of the parent or school. The IEP must include statements regarding the child's present levels of educational performance, annual goals, how these goals will be met in special and regular classrooms, and how achievement of these goals will be evaluated.

There are two major inputs that communication-oriented teachers can make at this point. One is facilitating the decision-making process among the participants in this meeting whose very diverse backgrounds and vested interests breed conflict. The full range of a teacher's knowledge and skill in interpersonal communication can be called for in this context.[1]

A second contribution is proposing ways to appropriately individualize the student's curriculum. These, too, are numerous, and can include the following: adapting curriculum goals, using textbooks on an appropriate level, tailoring classwork and homework assignments to achievement levels, changing the required mode of receiving information (students unable to read a text could listen to a taped version), changing the required mode of response (students with severe writing problems could answer questions orally), adapting instructions for assignments to make sure that they are understood, administering tests covering content adjusted to adapted curriculum goals, modifying the standard of grading, adjusting the expected standard of classroom behavior for students with behavioral or emotional problems, allowing more time to practice a new concept or skill for mastery, and adjusting the questions asked in class discussions to the level of understanding of students with learning problems.[2]

The next stage in mainstreaming is aiding the initial integration of the handicapped student into the regular classroom. Teachers begin this process by modeling awareness and acceptance of every individual's unique strengths and weaknesses, which include their own. They can admit that they themselves do not have the answers to every question and that all students are valued in spite of their problem areas and disabilities.

Student sensitivity to handicaps can be enhanced by using interaction procedures such as role playing. Students might be blindfolded for an hour, wear tight earmuffs for a day, or spend time in a wheelchair imagining what it would be like never to stand up. Impatience with a slow reader is reduced by giving students a textbook on a higher grade level or a foreign language book. Careful teacher guidance through these activities can help students experience and understand what it's like to walk in someone else's shoes for a while.

Teachers also can provide opportunities for handicapped students to demonstrate the abilities they do have and to assume positions of leadership in the classroom. Teachers might assist handicapped students in explaining the nature of their handicapping condition (particularly in the cases of visual, hearing, and physical impairments) to other class members and in facilitating a subsequent frank, open question–answer session in which individual differences are respected. Books, films, and guest speakers can be useful—e.g., handicapped adults can provide information about the positive contributions handicapped people have made to society. Pairing students into a buddy system has helped handicapped newcomers with their academic problems and with social interaction. Teachers need to provide initial guidance and monitoring for these dyads, even to make sure that the nonhandicapped peer is not being oversolicitous in an effort to be helpful and that the benefits are mutual—i.e., giving and receiving constitutes a two-way street between the two students.

Research indicates that normal children of elementary school age often ignore or ridicule learning disabled students. When this occurs, the teacher might reinforce, via demonstration or word, "Johnny's" right and ability to be in the class and then actively incorporate the handicapped student in classroom work groups.

Communication educators must be informed and sensitive about language use in regard to the handicapped. They should know what relevant terms such as *legal blindness* and *partial sightedness* refer to. Many educators have been found to regard all persons with hearing losses as "deaf" and to use terms like "deaf and dumb." The labels "feeble-minded," "idiot," "moron," "weak-minded," and "retarded" often are used interchangeably. Handicapped persons prefer that the appropriate descriptive terms be used as adjectives rather than nouns—i.e., *retarded* persons as opposed to *the retarded;* or *individuals with hearing impairment* rather than *the deaf.*

Parent–teacher communication is expanded when handicapped children are involved. Beginning at the IEP meeting, and throughout the year, they must share decision making about curriculum, class procedures, and homework. Other issues make interaction between them especially significant. For example, reporting student progress or grades can be a particularly sensitive area. Since many schools compute grades on a normal curve, those with learning problems often are at the bottom, their achievement falling below grade level. Conferences with parents make individual academic progress explicit and keep failing report card grades from crushing their enthusiasm. At these conferences other issues such as social interaction, physical activities, sexuality, etc., may need exploration as well.

A new interaction, between regular and special educators, also results from mainstreaming. Many special educators have had to emerge from their isolated classrooms and assume the role of *resource teachers.* They provide, and classroom teachers must use, their help in a new, flexible consultant role. Both now are asked to do what they "were not trained to do." This shift can cause anxiety, confusion, and resentment. These generate resistance, and an attitude of "it won't work" has pervaded many new mainstreaming programs. Unprecedented roles must be fashioned and new skills learned by everyone involved in an undertaking as profound as mainstreaming. Communication plays a major role in its introduction and acceptance in a school, and this contribution will be widely sought in the 1980's.

SHY OR RETICENT STUDENTS

During the 1970's much attention was given to a previously overlooked learning handicap: shyness or reticence. The quiet student was reinforced in traditional classrooms. Teachers were not aware of the problems that accompany inhibited communication until research revealed that the chances for habitually quiet individuals to succeed in school, job, and social interaction generally were diminished. School programs began to be developed for students who frequently have messages to share but who hesitate to do so. The students' subjective experiences were elicited, causes were explored, methods of identification were developed, and approaches to prevention and to treatment of reticence were devised.[3] These will be reviewed briefly here.

Subjective Experiences

Shy people see social situations as risky; they distrust their own ability to speak; they expect a negative evaluation from others; they experience physiological symptoms of stress before and during speaking; and they are more hesitant than nonshy students to be assertive in offering to help others, in disagreeing with others, and in speaking with authority figures.

Causes

The roots of shyness are hard to pin down. Among several hypotheses that have been made and have received some support are the following: the achievement judging orientation of contemporary society, high family mobility, little parent–child interaction, a norm of "children should be seen and not heard" at home and/or in school, ridicule during early school speaking experiences, minimal exposure to social situations (e.g., in a rural setting), and disparity between home and school interaction norms (e.g., one ethnic group predominates around the home and another at school).

Identification

Quietness alone does not always indicate shyness. Some quiet children prefer being reserved; others attempt to disguise shyness by feigning disinterest in socializing or by limiting themselves to only a few safe interaction contexts. Hence, a number of self-report scales have been developed. The most widely used with elementary and secondary students is the Personal Report of Communication Fear.[4]

Prevention

The first step in relieving shyness is to minimize the conditions under which it is most likely to occur. The incidence of shyness is higher in some social contexts than in others. Shyness is least likely to occur in classrooms where the following are characteristic: (1) students' comments are accepted rather than judged; (2) student interaction is encouraged; (3) learning is carried out through group activities; (4) activities are sequenced from those that are least threatening (e.g., group work) through those that maximize exposure (e.g., giving a speech); (5) the feelings that lie behind social interaction are discussed; (6) recommended approaches to oral activities are structured clearly and specifically so that students know exactly what to do; and (7) students are called on only for answers they can handle; many other preventative strategies are also used.[5]

Forms of Treatment

When students appear or report themselves to be shy, four general treatment strategies are available:

1. *Reducing anxiety*—Students can learn to reduce the physical tension that accompanies the act of speaking (systematic desensitization).

2. *Providing insight and understanding*—Students can change the inhibiting and inappropriate beliefs that come to mind during situations of shyness.

3. *Improving social skills*—Students can be taught specific strategies for being more assertive and rhetorically effective when speaking, and opportunities can be provided for practicing these skills.

4. *Altering self-perceptions*—Students can be encouraged to see more value in themselves and what they have to say.

Now that information about the need, causes, identification procedures, and preventive and treatment methods for shyness and reticence is available, it is likely that more attention will be given to this problem in the 1980's. Much interest already has been shown in popular workshops and publications. However, early intervention is necessary to handle the problem most effectively, and schools are the most appropriate setting for such intervention.

GIFTED STUDENTS (LEADERSHIP ABILITY)

In 1972 the U.S. Office of Education issued the Marland Report, which singled out *leadership ability* as a component of children's giftedness requiring "differential educational programs and services beyond those normally provided by the regular school program." By 1978 this recommendation had been included in legislation mandating special programs for gifted and talented students in 24 states. As a result, during the 1980's increased attention will be given to students gifted with potential leadership ability.

In order to develop programs suitable for nurturing leadership ability, we need to answer several questions: What is the purpose of such programs? How are students identified for them? What should be done in such programs? We will consider each here.

Purpose

Traditionally, competitive forensic events and elective courses in public speaking, drama, and mass media have been offered in secondary schools as vehicles for developing leadership ability. Contemporary views of leadership, however, stress the importance of face-to-face interaction in which the skills of listening, asserting, interviewing, group problem solving, confirming others, delegating responsibility, etc., are paramount. The development of leadership talent in the 80's, therefore, is likely to emphasize interpersonal communication.

Leadership theory, in the realm of interpersonal management and supervisory behavior, has come to stress a *contingency* approach—i.e., leaders each have inherent styles, so to be effective, each must be matched appropriately to the people and tasks s/he can deal with best. Thus, a leader's success depends upon her/his being placed in the right spot at the right time. A leader is most effective when dealing with "favorable" situations—i.e., those that lie within the limits of her/his habitual patterns of interaction.

Students, especially in early grades, may not as yet have developed a style of leadership. They still can be encouraged to transcend narrow patterns of interaction and to attain situational and stylistic flexibility —e.g., to be control-oriented at times, to be people-oriented at times). The purpose of early leadership training, therefore, is to develop *effective flexibility of social behavior.*

Identification

Students with leadership potential can be identified in several ways. One is through their accelerated development of interpersonal competencies. In earlier chapters synthesized lists are provided of competencies that characterize children at elementary and secondary levels. When these are noted earlier than expected in some children's behavior, those individuals can be selected for special attention and leadership instruction.

A second method involves peer nomination. Students can be assigned activities to carry out in groups. Afterward, they can be asked questions such as these:

1. Who most influenced the other participants? (You may include yourself when answering these questions.)

2. Who most clearly defined the problems?

3. Who offered the best solutions to the problems?

4. Who worked the hardest to get the job done and come to a good conclusion?

5. Who encouraged the others to participate?

6. Whom do you like best? (Do not include yourself on this one.)

7. Who tried to keep the group running smoothly and encouraged cooperation?

8. Overall, who was the "leader" in this group?

A third method is self-nomination. This can be achieved by giving students projective tasks—e.g., asking them to describe what is occurring in pictures depicting ambiguous social situations. Those who perceive issues of power or leadership in the pictures can be deemed most oriented in this direction. Also, students can be asked to describe what they would like their lives to be like in 20 years. Those who visualize leadership roles for themselves also might be included in the designated group.

Finally, speech communication and leadership abilities can be identified using standardized self-report instruments. For example, in the state of Idaho the following four measures are suggested to identify these individuals: The Barclay Classroom Climate Inventory, the Bonney-Fessondon Sociogram, the Junior–Senior High School Personality Questionnaire (for grades 7 through 12), and the Vineland Social Maturity Scale (for all ages).

Activities

Programs directed at students gifted in leadership ability need to have several qualities. They must enhance students' recognition of their own freedom of choice or potential for flexibility (a humanistic approach) *and* of the need to develop and practice the skills that must be used to achieve their social goals (a behavioral or rhetorical approach).

Their learning must occur in a supportive, understanding environment. Schools often label as "discipline problems" and penalize outgoing, independent individuals, thereby turning their leadership talents toward out-of-school, sometimes antisocial, activities.

Schools also must offer explicit instruction in leadership theory and methods, as well as provide for self-directed, experiential activities in which leadership abilities are developed through the trial-and-error of actual practice.

Special projects can provide opportunities for enriching regular classroom programs. Several that have been used are summer internships or apprenticeships with leaders in community organizations, serving as group discussion leaders for teachers of other subject areas, and the study of future trends and simulated problem solving for situations that might be faced by society in the years ahead.[6]

BILINGUAL/BICULTURAL STUDENTS

Concern about the pervasiveness of poor school performance among children whose first language is not English, and about their subsequent social and economic disadvantages, led to the passage of Title VII of the Elementary and Secondary Education Act, also known as the Bilingual Education Act. The basic definition of *bilingual education* (as stated by the U.S. Office of Education) is as follows:

> . . . the use of two languages, one of which is English, as mediums of instruction for the same pupil population in a well-organized program which encompasses part or all of the curriculum and includes the study of the history and culture associated with the mother tongue. A complete program develops and maintains the children's self-esteem and a legitimate pride in both cultures.

Due to legislation, recommendations made by the U.S. Commission on Civil Rights, and several major U.S. Supreme Court decisions (e.g., *Lau v. Nichols* and *Aspira of New York v. Board of Education*), this bilingual education process has been incorporated in public school systems having students of Cuban, Puerto Rican, Mexican, Native American, Chinese, Vietnamese, and other non-English backgrounds. However, despite its prevalence, much academic and political controversy surrounds bilingual education, and a review of the literature uncovers several hotly contested issues that concern students' and teachers' communication abilities:

1. To what extent should instruction be in the first language or mother tongue (L_1) or in the second or national language, English (L_2)?

2. What is the better sequencing of languages? Should initial literacy be taught in L_1 or L_2, or should they be taught simultaneously?

3. When should the second language be introduced? Most U.S. Department of Education Title VII programs introduce reading in L_2 simultaneously with L_1 or no more than one year later. Canadian programs (called *early immersion programs*) do not introduce reading in L_1 until second grade, after two years of schooling (K, 1).

4. What is the effect of each emphasis on the consequent achievement of language skills, especially initial reading, in both languages?

5. What are the effects of either emphasis on subject matter learning in fields such as mathematics and science and on general cognitive ability?

6. To what extent should cultural customs or social interactional rules of language use employed in L_1 and/or L_2 be emphasized in the program?

7. To what extent should teachers in bilingual programs be members of the L_1 ethnic group? To what extent do they need to be fluent in the language and familiar with the culture of L_2?

8. How are outcomes of such programs best measured? By students' performance on standardized tests in language arts, mathematics, and self-concept? By students' success in the mainstream culture—i.e., by school dropout rates, posteducation economic success, assimilation into the mainstream culture?

9. Is ethnic separatism a problem, a vestige of a primitive past, that must be overcome (the "melting pot" theory), or, as writers on the "new pluralism" have argued, are ethnic groups a basic component of our social structure that affect our institutions and are, at times, more powerful than economic forces in their influence?

10. Are schools the appropriate agency for dealing with the problem of unequal achievement and prosperity among minority groups? Or is it the case that because schools are only part of the ideological structure that a ruling class controls to maintain its dominance over the masses, and because schools are, there-

fore, dependent on the dominant economic and political institutions, they cannot be a primary agent of social transformation.

The answers to these questions are by no means resolved as we enter the second decade of bilingual education. A study can be found to support virtually every possible opinion. Frequently, debates over educational methodology actually have at their base differing commitments to political ideologies. In fact, Title VII funded programs officially eschew the use of the term *bilingual/bicultural education* (an HEW official has been quoted as saying, "The United States government is in the business to teach language, not to teach culture"[7]). In the midst of such controversy, caution is imperative.

Nevertheless, after acknowledging the controversies, direction emerges within bilingual education related to interpersonal communication that seems very likely to predominate in the 1980's. Whatever the intent, form, or methods used in such programs, the basic concern must remain the enhancing of two-way communication between members of the majority and minority groups. This process is not optimized through language or subject matter learning alone. Children raised in ethnic enclaves, whether suburban Anglos or barrio Chicanos, develop familiarity only with the sociolinguistic rules of their own group. To interact successfully with members of the "other" culture, each must develop competence in the alternative system as well. Teachers also must learn both sets of norms. They must be wary of misinterpreting their bilingual students' behavior because of contrasting interactional rules, as in the use of space, eye contact, or voice level, and in permitted speech acts —e.g., types of questions. Anglo teachers must not allow any kind of aberrant behavior from minority students out of misplaced cultural tolerance because they do not know what the acceptable norms are. They must make adjustments to the inclinations of their students and teach them through means to which they most readily adapt, *and* they also must teach them the ways of social interaction, in and out of school, that are acceptable in the dominant culture. The reverse is equally true —majority students must be taught the mores of the minority group(s) with whom they are likely to interact. Toward this end, a number of classroom techniques have been worked out that incorporate social interaction rules of the second culture into classroom practices.[8]

During the 1970's the utopian dreams of separatist and integrationist idealists collapsed. The lives of ethnic group members will continue to be interwoven with the mainstream culture, and they are unlikely to melt entirely and harmoniously into it. The communication-oriented teacher is likely to remain a valuable and more frequently tapped resource for facilitating this interaction in the years ahead.

FEMALE STUDENTS

During the 1970's a number of publications offered evidence of differences between male and female communication behavior and suggested that these differences affected the personal and professional lives of the members of both groups. These findings generally reveal a male-dominant communication norm. For example, women tend to speak less frequently than men in mixed groups and dyads, and are less apt to initiate topics of discussion; their topics are less likely to be developed; their unit speech time is less than men's; and men interrupt more than women.[9] Hence, the special emphasis has been on providing opportunities for women to expand their capacity to interact effectively in mixed-sex contexts. This concern has given rise to special courses dealing with male–female communication, to separate sections of traditional courses especially aimed at women, and to heightened attention to the participation of women within every classroom situation.

Some of the topics addressed when the influence of sex role on communication is discussed are as follows:

1. *Self-concept*—How have cultural and familial sex-role stereotypes shaped students' views of themselves and what they are able to do? Do females believe in their own ability to think logically, to organize, and to articulate their ideas?

2. *Interaction conditioning*—What are the unspoken "rules" of interaction between males and females? How are distinctions made between what is denigrated as *pushy* or *emasculating* and what is admired as *determined* or *forceful*?

3. *Disclosure*—What are the differences between what females and males share within same-sex groups and what is disclosed to members of the opposite sex? What fears are perpetuated by these limitations, and what misunderstandings occur as a result of the distorted impressions each receives?

4. *Assertiveness/receptivity*—How can females learn to affirm their beliefs, concerns, rights, preferences, etc., without muffling or minimizing (or imposing) them? How can they best handle the conflicts that may arise when old patterns of interaction are first broken?

5. *Media influence*—How do the language that is used and the visual images that appear on television and in films, newspapers, magazines, etc., affect perceptions of how females "should" behave?

6. *Relationships*—How are issues of intimacy and control usually worked out in male–female interaction? What alternatives are available for negotiating and implementing these dimensions of a relationship?

Even when the focus is not on the topic of social interaction, teachers can have an effect on female students' communication behavior. Teachers can provide support during instances when female students seem to minimize their capacity to do traditionally male activities (e.g., math, science, athletics), when they talk about future career plans or evidence fear of success, and when they back down on points on which they disagree with males in the class. Teachers can also encourage females to assume positions of leadership in group activities, they can use methods such as debate and role playing to provide female students with practice in articulating ideas, and they can highlight women's historical and current contributions to social progress.

CONCLUSION

The 1980's hold promise for taking some significant steps toward fulfilling the American dream of equal opportunity for all. The groundwork has been laid by legislators, lawyers, researchers, and others for handicapped, reticent, gifted, bilingual, and female students to realize their full potential. It is now the responsibility of teachers across the nation to carry on this work in their daily classroom interaction. This will be a challenging decade for all involved in this endeavor.

REFERENCES

1. Friedman, Paul G. *Communication in Conferences: Parent–Teacher–Student Interaction.* Falls Church, Va.: Speech Communication Association, 1980.

2. Paul, James L.; Turnbull, Ann P.; and Cruickshank, William. *Mainstreaming: A Practical Guide.* New York: Schocken Books, 1979. pp. 62–63.

3. Friedman, Paul G. *Shyness and Reticence in Students.* Washington, D.C.: National Education Association, 1980.

4. *Ibid.*

5. *Ibid.*

6. Friedman, Paul G. *Teaching the Gifted and Talented in Oral Communication and Leadership.* Washington, D.C.: National Education Association, 1980.

7. Paulson, Christina B. "Bilingual/Bicultural Education." *Review of Research in Education 6.* (Edited by Lee S. Shulman.) Itasca, Ill.: F. E. Peacock, 1979.

8. *Ibid.*

9. Eakins, Barbara, and Eakins, Gene R. *Sex Differences in Human Communication.* Boston: Houghton Mifflin, 1978.

Additional Readings

Eakins, Barbara, and Eakins, Gene R. *Sex Differences in Human Communication.* Boston: Houghton Mifflin Company, 1978. Reviews theory and research regarding how conversational style, words, voice, social norms, and nonverbal behavior affect communication between men and women and how each group views themselves and the opposite sex.

Friedman, Paul G. *Communicating in Conferences: Parent–Teacher–Student Interaction.* Falls Church, Va.: Speech Communication Association, 1980. Stages and strategies are discussed that are likely to arise in the course of conferences with students and/or their parents dealing with problems in the educational process. Exercises useful in applying these methods comprise the second half of the book.

———. *Shyness and Reticence in Students.* Washington, D.C.: National Education Association, 1980. Theory and research are summarized that are addressed to understanding the nature, prevention, and treatment of students who are quiet in school. Many classroom practices for diagnosing and dealing with their problems are provided.

———. *Teaching the Gifted and Talented in Oral Communication and Leadership.* Washington, D.C.: National Education Association, 1980. Characteristics of students who are gifted in social and leadership ability, and techniques for developing their talents are detailed in this volume. It provides a handbook for setting up a program addressed to meeting these students' special needs.

Paul, James L.; Turnbull, Ann P.; and Cruickshank, William M. *Mainstreaming: A Practical Guide.* New York: Schocken Books, 1979. pp. 62–63. The rationale of mainstreaming, its various manifestations, and means for implementing mainstreaming programs are discussed in this book. It provides the administrator's, the consulting teacher's, the classroom teacher's, the parent's, and the exceptional child's perspectives.

Paulson, Christina B. "Bilingual/Bicultural Education." *Review of Research in Education 6.* (Edited by Lee S. Shulman.) Itasca, Ill.: F.E. Peacock, 1979. Recent theory and research devoted to bilingual/bicultural education are summarized here. Controversies in the field are discussed; research needs are spotlighted; the future of this movement is foretold; and upcoming trends are hypothesized.

144

CHAPTER 18

Learning Styles

John A. Daly
Content Consultants: Jan Andersen
West Virginia University
Karen Garrison
Auburn University

Most people who spend any significant portion of their time thinking about education come to acknowledge that good teaching often requires that materials and instruction be adapted to differences among students. What is right for one student may not be appropriate for another: Some pupils flourish with one form of instruction; others blossom with another. This realization leads us to focus on student learning styles. Learning styles refer to broad, stable differences among people in how they best learn. Educational researchers have accumulated compelling evidence for the importance of these styles. And, as these findings mount, classroom teachers will want to consider more and more the role of learning styles in instructional activities. During the 80's, more and more research on these styles will reach the public's attention, leading to demands for greater teacher awareness of, and adaption to, these differences.

This chapter summarizes some of the major themes of research on learning styles. Initially some of the important approaches research has taken will be surveyed. Then the special needs of speech communication teachers will be focused on by identifying some potentially important learning style variables that may affect the success of speech communication instruction.

RESEARCH ON LEARNING STYLES

Differences in Intellectual Abilities

An immediately obvious group of learning style variables can be labeled as *intellectual abilities.* Some students are more able than others in academic pursuits. Research, for the most part, treats ability as a unitary student characteristic often specific to subject matter. The findings of a number of studies suggest that students with strong abilities fare better than those with weak abilities. Beyond this almost trivial claim are findings that specific instructional techniques affect high and low ability students differently. High ability pupils, for example, prefer learning environments that offer few rules. Their low ability counterparts perform better in more structured settings. Also, rote drills help the performance of low ability pupils, yet hinder the performance of high ability ones who quickly get bored with the unnecessary practice. High ability students perform better with hypothesis generation exercises that require synthesis.

Some recent research moves beyond the unitary ability framework and identifies multiple clusters of intellectual ability. The broadest grouping, devised by Lee Cronbach and Richard Snow of Stanford University, includes three variables: fluid–analytic abilities that are reflected in abstract reasoning tasks, crystallized–verbal abilities that are represented by most verbal and educational tests, and spatial–visual abilities that are shown by a student's skill at visualizing spatial relationships.[1] Too little research has been completed to date on these three clusters to permit any broad generalizations. However, the implications of this tripartite are numerous. Notably, the orientation is away from subject-specific abilities and toward more cognitive differences that cross disciplinary boundaries. Also, a student may vary independently on each of the three dimensions, thus eliminating any standard of general ability.

A new concern in research on multiple abilities is with the role of the two brain hemispheres.[2] While the research on hemispheric differences is complex and incomplete, a few generalizations can be made and applied to instruction. First, the brain is differentiated in terms of tasks. The left side of the brain is most active when tasks require predominantly verbal and analytic skills. The right side is associated more with spatial and imagery activities. This difference is often assessed by measuring the amount of electrical activity occurring on each side of the brain during performance of some task that varies in its demand for spatial and verbal activities. Second, there are differences between males and females in hemispheric processes. Females are more integrated insofar as they tend to use both parts of the brain on most tasks. Males tend to allow one hemisphere or the other to dominate. Third, people differ in the way they best learn. Some students are better with analytic or verbal materials (their left side dominates); others are best with spatial or imagery materials (their right side dominates). Most school teachers, according to some authorities, are biased toward students with a dominant left side. Subjects are taught, and assessments designed, in an analytic–verbal fashion. This bias may preclude right-dominant pupils from gaining or evidencing knowledge. Yet, teachers could adapt their materials and units to these differences. There are more ways to teach a unit than most teachers realize.

Differences in Learning Modalities and Processes and Types of Learners

At variance with the intellectual abilities orientation is research on *process, modality, and type* differences among students in how they go about learning. The research of R.R. Schmeck and Eddie Grove serves as an example of process approaches.[3] They, along with colleagues, have spent the last few years developing a construct and measure that tap four dimensions of the learning process. The first, called *synthesis–analysis,* refers to students' tendencies to process information either superficially or deeply. The more deeply students process incoming information, the better their academic performance, prose and verbal learning, critical thinking, and note-taking efficiency. *Elaborative processes,* the second dimension, are associated with pupils' abilities to translate information into personal references—that is, making personal sense of, and, in fact, elaborating on, the information presented. It is contrasted with verbatim processing of information in which students simply take in the immediate stimulus information without extension or elaboration. This dimension is related to imagery ability, learning, and college performance. *Fact retention* is the third dimension. It is concerned with students' proclivities to pay attention to, and process, details and specifics of stimuli instead of taking in only broad generalities. It is related to learning and college performance. The final dimension, *study methods,* does not correlate well with learning. Students high in this dimension study through drill and practice rather than thoughtful analysis. They apparently intend to learn but fail in their efforts. While Schmeck and his colleagues don't directly consider teaching adaptions that would maximize student learning with pupils varying in each of the four dimensions, the implications are obvious. Students process information differently, and their instruction should be adapted to these differences when it can.

Other research emphasizes modality differences in learning. Studies have demonstrated that students may vary in their abilities to learn from auditory or visual presentations of information. Auditory learners do better when materials are presented orally; visual learners do better with visual presentation.

In addition, some investigations have focused on types of learners. Pupils are differentiated along a continuum according to how they respond to instruction. Typical of this approach is M.B. Rosenberg's framework in which he posits four learning styles along a single dimension. The first is called *rigidity*. Students in this category have difficulty with complex materials, are often dogmatic with low tolerance for ambiguity, and possess little creativity. The second level is termed *undisciplined.* Students here are marked by impulsiveness, low goal orientations, and an inability to tolerate frustration or delay gratification. *Acceptance–anxiety* is the third group. Pupils classified in this cluster are very concerned with how others evaluate them. They are low in intrinsic motivation and dependent on others for acceptance. The final level is labeled *creative.* Learners in this group are self-confident, independent, and original. Measures assessing each of these dimensions have been devised by psychologist Karl Neumann and his associates.[4]

Differences in Cognitive Style

A third approach to learning styles is exemplified by investigations of *cognitive style.* Cognitive style refers to the ways people conceptually organize their environments. The style construct is actually an aggregation of four personality variables: complexity, field dependence–independence, rigidity, and locus of control. Because each of these variables may have implications for instruction, it is useful to consider them individually.

Complexity is a multifaceted variable emphasizing differences among people in their cognitive structures.[5] People may represent their worlds in terms of constructs that serve to organize how they interpret and respond to objects and events. For any stimulus, people differ in the number of constructs they generate. Those who arrive at many are considered more *differentiated* than those who come up with only a few. Some people also interrelate their constructs about an event or object in complex ways: They see many relationships among them. They are more *integrative* than those who don't see as many relationships.

People low in differentiation and integration are, in complexity terms, *concrete.* Others who are high on the two dimensions are *abstract.* Abstract students do better on essay exams requiring comparisons and contrasts than do concrete pupils. Both do equally well on multiple choice exams. Students high in abstraction ask more questions than do their more concrete counterparts, and, when the environment is controlled for complexity, they prefer complex messages to simple ones—just the opposite of what concrete subjects want.

Field dependence–independence refers to the degree to which a person depends on external and environmental cues in interpreting events and objects.[6] Some people need and use many situational cues to make sense of a stimulus object or event. They are *dependent* on the field. Others, called *field independents,* pay less attention to the environmental field. Research finds that field dependent students learn materials with social content better than do field independents. This is not because of greater intellectual abilities; rather, field dependent pupils selectively attend more to social stimuli. Field independents are better at learning materials that require them to provide their own organization or structure; field dependents like to have materials presented within a pre-established structure. Field independent students are more intrinsically motivated, while field dependent pupils are more concerned with external criticism. Some evidence also exists to suggest that field independent students prefer subjects such as mathematics, while field dependent students like subjects that are more socially oriented such as communication. Again, the effective classroom teacher who recognizes that his or her students differ along this dimension would be well advised to adopt differing teaching practices.

Rigidity refers to a group of very similar variables that emphasize how structured and rigid a person is.[7] Included are authoritarianism, dogmatism, and intolerance of ambiguity. Authoritarianism, for the most part, has been supplanted in the psychological literature by the dogmatism construct. The original measure of authoritarianism, the F Scale, was limited in what it assessed; it had strong tendencies to assess only right-wing authoritarian responses. This, along with other criticisms, led to the development of a similar, but more general, construct called *dogmatism.* Dogmatic people are considered more closed-minded, responsive to authority, and polarized than are nondogmatic people. Dogmatists are less able to distinguish source from message. Their evaluations of statements are related to their evaluations of the people making the statements. In the classroom, dogmatic people may have difficulty separating an instructional unit from their feelings about the teacher. They are also less tolerant of ambiguity. People with a low tolerance for ambiguity prefer straightforward, unambiguous, and consistent stimuli presentations; they balk at events and objects that demand an acceptance of ambiguity.

Locus of control is typically considered a cognitive personality variable.[8] It emphasizes the extent to which people believe events happening to them are dependent on their own behavior or, instead, are the result of luck, fate, chance, or other things beyond their personal control. People with an internal locus of control see themselves as controlling their own fates, while externals feel that their fates are not under their control. Internals conform less to influence attempts, are more task centered, and are dependent on their own abilities and skills. They typically outperform externals on cognitive tasks and generally do better in academic work. Perhaps these differences in classroom performance are due to the demand most academic work places on students to demonstrate some responsibility for their effort. Teachers recognizing these differences can modify their talk, assignments, instructions, and discussions to adjust to the differing frames that their students take. And, by modifying reinforcement contingencies, teachers may be able to affect their students' locus of control.[9]

Differences in Noncognitive Variables

A final approach to learning styles involves research on more *noncognitive personality* variables that affect how students learn. Only two variables will be briefly discussed here. The first is *anxiety*. The extensive research that has been completed on this disposition[10] suggests, for example, that anxious students prefer teacher-centered instruction, while their nonanxious peers favor more student-centered approaches in the classroom (however, there are some methodological concerns about these findings).[11] The second noncognitive variable is *the way in which pupils approach achievement.* Some students emphasize achievement through conformity; others seek achievement through independence. The use of instructional styles matching these different approaches can result in better learning. Many other variables fit within this noncognitive, personality approach. Among them are orientation toward competition and cooperation, reward orientation, introversion–extroversion, level of aspiration, and need for achievement.

LEARNING STYLES IN COMMUNICATION INSTRUCTION

The learning styles described have implications across virtually every academic subject. Certainly they can be applied to differentiating instruction in oral communication. In addition, a few specific variables that may be central to how students perform in communication classes but that haven't been mentioned so far will be described here.

One major variable that affects students in speech communication classes is *anxiety about oral communication.*[12] Communication journals are dotted with research on the topic ranging from considerations of stage fright and speech anxiety to the broader concerns of communication apprehension, reticence, and social anxiety. On a very general level, this variable refers to a student's willingness to comfortably engage in oral communication activities. Students who are low in the anxiety enjoy communication experiences; those who are more anxious don't like them. Research indicates that highly anxious students do less well in discussion and seminar classes than do their low anxious peers. However there is no performance difference between the two groups in lecture classes. High and low anxious pupils also vary in how they interpret communication activities. Low anxious ones see them as rewarding; high anxious pupils see them as punishing. Generally, more anxious students avoid interaction in the classroom by not talking and by choosing seatings that do not draw attention to themselves. They differ, as well, from nonanxious students in the quality and quantity of oral presentations. Being aware of this difference can facilitate effective teaching of communication. For instance, not all students will profit equally from required communication activities: Low anxious students may; high anxious ones probably won't.

Researchers in social psychology work with a construct they call *self-awareness* or *self-consciousness*. [13] It refers to people's tendencies to focus attention on themselves. Some people pay lots of attention to themselves as social objects; others don't. Much communication instruction is based on self-reflection and self-criticism of one's communication attempts. Students are asked, for instance, to think about how they communicate, about how others are looking and listening to them— essentially, to pay attention to themselves as social objects. Highly self-aware pupils may interpret and internalize these exercises better than do those who spend little time in self-reflection.

Psychologist Mark Snyder has devised a construct called *self-monitoring* [14] that may have direct relevance to teachers concerned with how students learn communication. Self-monitoring concerns the abilities that people have to control and to manage their behavior in the presence of others. High self-monitors are sensitive to expressions and self-presentations of others; they use these cues to guide them in choosing and monitoring their own verbal and nonverbal behaviors. By contrast, low self-monitors don't pay much attention to others' cues; they are less able to control their social moves to fit the situation. High self-monitors use the situation to guide them; low self-monitors more often let their internal states affect them. This seems especially relevant for the communication classroom. Audience adaptation demands an awareness of audience cues. Some students may be better than others at recognizing and adjusting to them. Similarly, in nonverbal skill development the ability to correctly interpret what another is signalling is critical to success. People differing in self-monitoring differ in their ability to read such cues. Enhancing students' abilities to communicate may require an adjustment for their level of self-monitoring.

Nonverbal sensitivity is a fourth variable that may have profound effects on how a student goes about learning communication skills. This topic has received a great deal of attention from a number of scholars, most recently and notably Robert Rosenthal and his colleagues.[15] They have devised a test to assess a person's sensitivity to nonverbal cues. The research to date suggests a number of things: Females are more sensitive than males; as children get older, their abilities to decode get better; at younger ages the greater a child's social sensitivity and extroversion, the better he/she is at decoding. In the communication classroom some students may be very sensitive to the nonverbal cues of peers and teacher; they interpret them well. Others may not be very good at this. While it can be taught (and perhaps should be in the communication classroom), most teachers will only be able to recognize that not all students are equally competent in interpreting the nonverbal nuances that so often carry much meaning in oral exchanges.

CONCLUSION

This chapter has surveyed some of the major approaches that research into learning styles has taken. It has also identified a group of variables that may be especially relevant to communication instruction. Other approaches, and other variables, could have been mentioned as well; but space limitations, as well as a desire to avoid a "shopping center" mentality about style research, preclude their selection.

What should communication teachers do about style differences in their classrooms? Three steps seem reasonable. First, psychologically accept that students vary in the ways they best learn. Many teachers seem to carry with them a belief that there is only one correct way to teach or learn something. That isn't true in any subject, especially communication. Second, recognize important learning style differences in the classroom. Through assessment, observation, and other means, identify variables that contribute to how well students learn materials. Those potential variables that have been mentioned here should give the interested teacher a taste of the number of styles potentially present in any classroom. Third, devise strategies that adapt teaching and materials to the specific learning needs of students. Aside from the specific adaptations related to one style or another suggested above, a few general strategies can be outlined.

One such strategy centers on the development of individually oriented instructional programs. Most popular among these approaches is the personalized system of instruction (PSI).[16] PSI emphasizes the individual learning needs of students. It allows pupils to progress at their own rates and highlights success rather than failure. It has been applied to communication instruction at a number of institutions of higher education. Most of these applications could easily be adapted to elementary and secondary levels. A second approach is far more basic in what it emphasizes. Labeled *learning strategies,* this approach centers on how instructors can modify their individual behaviors and materials to bring about optimal learning. A recently published text edited by Harold O'Neil summarizes much of the current research.[17] A final approach may be the blandest, but also the most general. Teachers can simply experiment with their own teaching styles to see which are the most effective with different types of students. The ultimate aim of learning styles research is the optimization of fit between the teacher's teaching style and the student's learning style. Teachers can emphasize multiple but simultaneous instructional approaches, observing their differential impact of students. Given some effort and time, optimal teaching techniques may emerge that are adapted to both the individual teacher and the subject matter. This approach can be accomplished in the everyday world of a teacher's classroom. It is obviously difficult—but the payoff of better learning is, of course, what teaching is all about. The decade of the 80's demands improved instruction. And what better way to provide it than adapting to student differences.[18]

REFERENCES

1. Cronbach, L., and Snow, R. *Aptitudes and Instructional Methods.* New York: Irvington, 1977.

2. Bogen, J.E. "Some Educational Implications of Hemispheric Specialization." *The Human Brain.* (Edited by Merl Wittrock.) Englewood Cliffs, N.J.: Prentice-Hall, 1977.

3. Schmeck, R.R., and Grove, E. "Academic Achievement and Individual Differences in Learning Processes." *Applied Psychological Measurement* 3: 43–50; 1979.

4. Neumann, K.F.; Barton, J.W.; and Critelli, J.W. "Factor Analysis of a System of Students' Learning Styles." *Perceptual and Motor Skills* 48: 723–728; 1979.

5. Goldstein, K.M., and Blackman, S. *Cognitive Style.* New York: John Wiley, 1978.
Scott, W.A.; Osgood, D.W.; and Peterson, C. *Cognitive Structure: Theory and Measurement of Individual Differences.* Washington, D.C.: V.H. Winston & Sons, 1979.

6. Witkin, H.A., and others. "Field-Dependent and Field-Independent Cognitive Styles and Their Educational Implications." *Review of Educational Research* 47: 1–64; 1977.

7. Goldstein, K.M., and Blackman, S. *op. cit.*

8. Lefcourt, H.M. *Locus of Control.* Hillsdale, N.J.: Lawrence Erlbaum, 1976.

9. Lepper, Mark R., and Grene, David, editors. *The Hidden Costs of Reward.* New York: Halsted Press, 1978.

10. See, for example: Sieber, J.E.; O'Neil, H.F.; and Tobias, S., editors, *Anxiety, Learning, and Instruction.* Hillsdale, N.J.: Lawrence Erlbaum, 1977.

11. Cronbach, L., and Snow, R. *op. cit.*

12. McCroskey, J.C. "Oral Communication Apprehension." *Human Communication Research* 4: 78–96; 1977.

13. Wicklund, R.A. "Objective Self-Awareness." *Advances in Experimental Social Psychology.* (Edited by Leonard Berkowitz.) New York: Academic Press, 1975. Vol. 8.

14. Snyder, M. "Self-Monitoring Processes." *Advances in Experimental Social Psychology.* (Edited by Leonard Berkowitz.) New York: Academic Press, 1979. Vol. 12.

15. Rosenthal, R., and others. *Sensitivity to Nonverbal Communication.* Baltimore: Johns Hopkins, 1979.

16. Sherman, J.G., editor. *Personalized System of Instruction.* Menlo Park, Calif.: W.A. Benjamin, 1974.

Scott, M.D., and Young, T.J. "Personalizing Communication Instruction." *Communication Education* 25: 211–221; 1976.

17. O'Neil, Harold, editor. *Learning Strategies.* New York: Academic Press, 1978.

18. William Seiler made many useful comments about this chapter. Gratefully I acknowledge his assistance.

Additional Readings

Bloom, Benjamin S. *Human Characteristics and School Learning.* New York: McGraw-Hill, 1976. This book reviews and develops a theory of the role of individual differences in instruction. It emphasizes the conditions necessary for effective learning as they interact with student differences.

Communication Education 25, March 1976. This issue of the journal presents articles on teaching the basic course in oral communication. There are two articles directly relevant to devising courses that stress the individual and his or her specific needs as they relate to communication.

Cronbach, Lee, and Snow, Richard. *Aptitudes and Instructional Methods.* New York: Irvington, 1977. This book has already become a classic critical review of educational research that stresses the interaction between learner characteristics and instructional methods. A must for the person interested in delving deeply into the research, it is, however, very technical in parts.

Goldstein, Kenneth M., and Blackman, Sheldon. *Cognitive Style: Five Approaches and Relevant Research.* New York: John Wiley, 1978. This text summarizes research on cognitive differences that may be relevant to education. The book is divided into sections on rigidity, dogmatism, complexity, and field dependence. A comprehensive view of the major approaches, theories, measurement techniques, and applied findings.

Sieber, Joan E.; O'Neil, Harold F.; and Tobias, Sigmund, editors. *Anxiety, Learning, and Instruction.* Hillsdale, N.J.: Lawrence Erlbaum, 1977. This edited text contains a number of articles relating student anxiety to instructional approaches. Its focus on anxiety provides a prototypical example of research approaches to the role of an individual difference in instruction.

CHAPTER 19

Instructional Strategies in the 80's

Gustav W. Friedrich
Content Consultants: Jan Andersen
West Virginia University
William D. Brooks
Oklahoma University

Previous chapters have focused on predicting content or subject matter changes for speech communication instruction in the 1980's and on describing the students and the settings for such instruction. This chapter concentrates on describing available instructional strategies—that is, repeatable instructional processes that are applicable across subject matters and that are useable by more than one teacher. The focus, then, is on identifying methods of teaching that are equally useful, for example, to teachers of interpersonal communication at the secondary level and to teachers of oral interpretation at the community college level.

In identifying such strategies, the focus will be on classroom teaching: a single teacher and a group of 20 to 40 students of approximately equal age. Given a current average of approximately 30 students per class and the current political climate for school finances, no radical changes in class size can be expected. When coupled with a forecasted 19 percent national decline in the number of 18-year-olds between 1980 and 1990, the prospects for new buildings are also slight. Thus, despite the fact that over 50 percent of all schools built from 1967 to 1970 were open space (generally characterized by a lack of interior walls and by the existence of instructional areas ranging in size from two ordinary classrooms to over 30), most classroom instruction in the 1980's is likely to occur within the context of the traditional "egg-crate" building. Thus, teachers in the 1980's are likely to teach approximately 30 students in a rectangular room containing a desk for the teacher and a small desk for each student, surrounded by windows, chalkboards, and bulletin boards, and with tile or wood floors. Within such a context it will be the teacher's task to find ways in which the various instructional strategies, each with its own advantages for different purposes and different students, can be most efficiently and effectively utilized.

In organizing this discussion of alternative instructional strategies, it is useful to think in terms of the three basic forms of activities that occur in the classroom:

1. *Extended discourse*—The teacher is talking, performing, demonstrating, or exhibiting materials. Lecturing accounts for between 18 and 22 percent of all class time.

2. *Interactive discourse*—The teacher and students are talking with each other. The degree of teacher control varies. Interactive discourse accounts for between 34 and 53 percent of all class time.

3. *Individual work*—The student is working on her or his own. Individual work accounts for between 25 and 45 percent of all class time.[1]

EXTENDED DISCOURSE

The most common form of extended discourse is the lecture method. It is also the most criticized. McLeish traces that criticism as far back as the Middle Ages when individuals criticized the "reading off" of lectures as an anachronism that should not have survived the invention of printing *(circa* 1440).[2] The critics' most common theme was that with the lecture method, the student is passive and limited to note taking, which reduces active contact with the curriculum. The lecture method has not lacked for defenders, however, who have pointed out that lectures give a framework, provide a point of view and information not otherwise available, and can kindle enthusiasm for a subject and stimulate original thinking. When combined with the fact that the lecture is adaptable, flexible, and inexpensive, it is small wonder that it continues to survive as one of the most frequently used instructional strategies. A variant of the lecture method that has the added advantages of interest and information is the guest lecturer or resource person.

A form of extended discourse that was widely touted as the panacea for the educational ills of the 1950's is television. After over a decade of well-controlled studies, however, the superiority of teaching traditional courses via television has yet to be demonstrated. McKeachie and Kulik argue that the major reason for this is that most instruction has conceptual rather than visual aims and, to learn to think conceptually, students need to interact with other human beings who can respond critically and helpfully to their conceptualizations.[3] In the 1980's, then, it is likely that television will be used in the speech classroom primarily as a medium for delivering short segments of instruction (when a clear visual image is important for learning or when the teacher wishes to build or raise student affect for content material) and for providing video playback of oral communication performances.

Possessing the potential to increase learning via extended discourse is Ausubel's subsumption theory of learning. Basically, this theory suggests that learning is facilitated by identifying a superordinate set of concepts already in students' memories that can be used to assist them in the assimilation of new material. Within the theory, advanced organizers and sequencing of instruction are variables that play central roles in effecting the assimilation of instructional material into a learner's schema.[4]

INTERACTIVE DISCOURSE

While extended discourse is a more efficient mode of presenting new information to students already motivated to learn, interactive discourse is more useful when the learning goals concern higher-level thinking, attitudes, and motivation. The most common type of interactive discourse is the developmental discussion—a term used to describe an approach by which students are assisted in finding their own concepts, principles, and solutions rather than receiving them from a teacher or a textbook.

Discussion methods range from recitation, in which the instructor asks specific questions in an oral quiz, to nondirective methods, in which the instructor says very little and students determine the topic and content of discussion. The following are among the special forms of discussion teaching

1. *Buzz groups*—Classes are split into small subgroups for a brief discussion of a problem and then asked to report back to the class.

2. *Student panel/student reports*—Students present reports or discuss a topic in front of fellow class members.

3. *Role playing*—Students are placed in relatively unstructured situations in which they must improvise behaviors to fit in with their concepts of the roles to which they have been assigned.

4. *Case method*—Students are provided with a factual written record of a situation, condition, and/or experience, and are asked to solve problems using knowledge, concepts, and skills that may have been learned in previous courses or that they are motivated by the case to learn from readings, lectures, or other resources.

5. *Simulation/gaming*—Students are involved in some sort of competition or achievement in relationship to a goal, a game that both teaches and is fun. When games attempt to model some real-life problem situation, they are called *simulations.*

A somewhat unique approach to organizing a course in terms of student interaction has been labeled *Guided Design.*[5] As a method, it involves dividing students into groups of four to seven and having them work through a series of increasingly complex, open-ended problems according to a prespecified series of decision-making steps. At the conclusion of each step, members of the work group are provided with teacher-written instructions—feedback material that guides them to a "model" solution. In the process students learn both the content of the course and how to use that content to solve realistic problems.

Because interactive discourse shares with the lecture method the advantages of adaptability, flexibility, and inexpensiveness, and because it is applicable to a wider variety of learning goals, interactive discourse in its many forms is likely to continue to predominate as an instructional strategy in the 1980's.

INDIVIDUAL WORK

Graded classes and lockstep group instruction replaced the country-school practices of individual recitation and peer teaching toward the end of the nineteenth century as publicly financed, compulsory elementary and secondary education became the norm. While the approach was administratively manageable and economically feasible, it proved difficult from the beginning to cope with the fact that groups are never really homogeneous. Scores of variables differentiate members of a particular grade with respect to maturity, intelligence, socioeconomic background, motivational drive, health, physical strength, sociability, creativity, perseverance, and emotional stability, to name but a few of the personal characteristics that affect learning. As a result, Charles

Eliot, president of Harvard, was only one of many to suggest in the 1890's that "uniformity is the curse of American schools."[6] Almost from the beginning of the graded approach to education, then, educational reformers were looking for ways to individualize instruction. Two of the more noteworthy attempts were the Winnetka Plan and the Dalton Plan. In the Winnetka Plan, used in Winnetka, Illinois, from 1919 to the early 1940's, each student was given a course of study for each subject in the program, and provision was made for continuous progress promotion of pupils on a nongraded basis. The Dalton Plan, used in the Dalton (Massachusetts) High School from 1920 to the mid-1930's, gave students a series of subjects to learn within a given block of time, typically 20 days. While students could individually pace themselves through each of the subjects, they needed to complete a comparable level of work in all subjects before moving on to the next level.

Attempts to individualize instruction are as prevalent today as they have ever been. Among some of the more common strategies being attempted are the following:

1. *Programmed instruction*—B.F. Skinner's prescription for curing the ills of teaching and learning in our schools; it consists of a system whereby each student—
   a. is presented with content (relatively brief presentations of about a sentence or a paragraph of instructional material)
   b. is required to respond actively (correctly answer a question or solve a problem)
   c. immediately thereafter receives information as to the correctness of the response.

   During the 1960's programmed textbooks and teaching machines proliferated, producing materials on such topics as parliamentary procedure, listening, and the organization of a speech. During the 1970's enthusiasm for the approach declined, however, as research accumulated demonstrating that while programmed instruction may be effective for response learning, ordinary reading is faster and more efficient for conceptual learning. In the 1980's, therefore, programmed instruction is likely to find its major use within units of a course when an instructor wishes students to master a particular skill or concept.

2. *Peer group instruction*—Students have been used to teach students in a variety of settings as a means of keeping classes small without an increase in cost. In 1963 Ohio University, for example, implemented a peer group instruction program and devel-

oped an extensive research program to investigate its effectiveness. In their application of this approach, teachers lectured simultaneously to two sections of a public speaking course, and students were responsible for rating one-half of the public speaking performances given in class. When Wiseman and Barker compared students in peer group instruction classes with those in traditional classes, they found no difference in terms of either performance or attitudinal outcomes.[7]

3. *Independent study*—This approach provides students with supervised experience in learning independently and with options for achieving course goals. In one variant of the approach, the student and teacher work out a set of goals to be achieved, methods of achieving the goals, and methods of evaluating achievement of the goals. A learning contract is then used to confirm that if achievement is at the agreed-upon level, the teacher will give the grade contracted for. In addition to the advantages of individualized instruction, the approach provides for increased motivation as a result of allowing students a voice in determining their course of study.

4. *Module approach*—This approach consists of reducing a course to modules or minicourses, and allowing students options in selecting among and/or pacing themselves through the modules. Brooks and Leth have used such an approach for the basic communication course at Purdue University; they report both greater achievement and more positive course and instructor evaluations when their approach is compared to traditional instruction.[8]

5. *Computer-aided instruction*—Although computers are being used as instructional devices, for testing, and as a means of record keeping, they have not yet reached the potential so long claimed for this form of instructional technology. For the moment, hardware has outstripped educational uses as minicomputers and microcomputers proliferate. Signs that this may not continue to be the case in the 1980's, however, are beginning to emerge. Lashbrook and Lashbrook, for example, have developed techniques for the computer simulation and analysis of audiences and for the analysis of small-group interaction.[9] The 1980's may well see computer-aided instruction come of age.

An approach that integrates elements from all of the above approaches is the Keller Plan, also called the Personalized System of Instruction (PSI). Within this approach, a course is divided into smaller units and students study each unit and then take a test on it. If students pass the test, they go on to the next unit. While PSI has many variations, it is characterized by five features:

1. It is individually paced—that is, a student, within the limits of administrative convenience, can proceed as quickly or slowly as s/he wants to.

2. It is mastery oriented—that is, a student continues a cycle of studying/testing, studying/testing until the criterion for acceptable work has been reached.

3. It is student tutored—that is, students who have successfully completed the course are available to help students enrolled in the course.

4. It uses printed guides for communication of information—that is, study guides are used to state objectives for the unit, offer suggestions for study, point out available resources, describe possible projects, and provide sample test items.

5. It is supplemented with traditional instructional techniques—that is, lectures, movies, etc., are scheduled for stimulation and/or clarification, but attendance at such sessions is usually voluntary.

Summarizing 75 studies that have compared PSI to other forms of instruction, Kulik and others conclude that not only do students like PSI better but also they learn more from it.[10] For example, scores on PSI final exams average about 8 percentage points higher, raising the final exam grade of a typical student from the 50th to the 70th percentile. When exams are administered several months after the end of the course, PSI has a 14-percentage-point advantage.

SUMMARY

Speech communication instruction in the 1980's is likely to be heavily dependent on forms of interactive discourse (especially developmental discussion and simulation/gaming) and the lecture for its instructional strategies because of their adaptability, flexibility, and inexpensiveness. Attempts to individualize instruction within the context of classroom teaching will probably continue, with variations of PSI likely to predominate. The 1980's may also be the decade in which computer-aided instruction achieves its promise as a form of instructional technology.

REFERENCES

1. Nuthall, Graham, and Snook, Ivan. "Contemporary Models of Teaching." *Second Handbook of Research on Teaching.* (Edited by R.W.M. Travers.) Chicago: Rand McNally, 1973. pp. 47–76.

2. McLeish, John. "The Lecture Method," *The Psychology of Teaching Methods.* (Edited by N.L. Gage.) Chicago: University of Chicago Press, 1976. pp. 252–301.

3. McKeachie, Wilbert J., and Kulik, James A. "Effective College Teaching." *Review of Research in Education 3.* (Edited by F.M. Kerlinger.) Itasca, Ill.: F.E. Peacock, 1975. pp. 165–209.

4. Mayer, Richard E. "Twenty Years of Research on Advance Organizers: Assimilation Theory Is Still the Best Predictor of Results." *Instructional Science* 8: 133–167; 1979.

5. Wales, Charles E., and Stager, Robert A. *Guided Design.* 1977. (Available from Charles E. Wales, West Virginia University, Morgantown, W.V. 26505)

6. Krug, Edward A., editor. *Charles W. Eliot and Popular Education.* New York: Teachers College, Columbia University, 1961. pp. 55–56.

7. Wiseman, Gordon, and Barker, Larry. "Peer Group Instruction: What Is It?" *Speech Teacher* 15: 220–223; September 1966.

8. Brooks, William D., and Leth, Pamela J. "Reducing Instructional Costs: A Survey of the Basic Course in Communication and an Experimental Test of a Proposed Instructional Model." *Communication Education* 25: 191–202; September 1976.

9. Lashbrook, William B., and Lashbrook, Velma J. *PROANA5: A Computerized Technique for the Analysis of Small Group Interaction User's Manual.* Minneapolis: Burgess Publishing Co., 1974.

10. Kulik, James A.; Kulik, Chen-Lin C.; and Cohen, Peter A. "A Meta-Analysis of Outcome Studies of Keller's Personalized System of Instruction." *American Psychologist* 34: 307–318; April 1979.

Additional Readings

Friedman, Paul G. *Interpersonal Communication: Innovations in Instruction.* Washington, D.C.: National Education Association, 1978. Explores the theoretical bases for the study and practice of the human relations approach to interpersonal communication. It also contains instructional approaches, teaching strategies, and numerous classroom activities.

Gage, N.L., editor. *The Psychology of Teaching Methods: Seventy-Fifth Yearbook,* Part I, National Society for the Study of Education. Chicago: University of Chicago Press, 1976. A collection of essays on teaching methods.

Johnson, Kent R., and Ruskin, Robert S. *Behavioral Instruction: An Evaluative Review.* Washington, D.C.: American Psychological Association, 1977. A synthesis of the literature on behavioral instruction which presents a state of the art and suggests directions for future research and for implementation of such approaches at the college level.

McKeachie, Wilbert J. *Teaching Tips: A Guidebook for the Beginning College Teacher.* Seventh edition. Lexington, Mass.: Heath, 1978. A survey of research related to teaching methods and other issues that face beginning college teachers.

Milton, Ohmer. *On College Teaching: A Guide to Contemporary Practices.* San Francisco: Jossey-Bass, 1978. A collection of essays on major teaching practices currently used in undergraduate education.

CHAPTER 20

The Training of Teachers

Ann Q. Staton-Spicer
Content Consultants: Ronald E. Bassett
University of Texas at Austin
Cassandra L. Book
Michigan State University

INTRODUCTION

The education of teachers is entwined with the values of society and, as such, is reflective of the times. As we move through the decade of the 1980's, two important conditions influence the direction of teacher training. First, education costs escalate year after year,[1] while public willingness to finance education declines. The passage of legislation such as Proposition 13 in California is evidence of a reluctance on the part of taxpayers to meet the financial needs of education. Second, there is still a surplus of teachers in many fields at the same time that school enrollments are falling.[2] One would assume, then, that given this surplus, the teachers who are hired are the most qualified and potentially effective. But this assumption has been questioned, given the nationwide decline in student test scores. Parents are disillusioned by the number of students who can neither read nor write, and they are beginning to cry "fraud" in much the same manner that consumers of material goods have done. This meshing of consumerism and education has resulted in parents' suing schools that have granted high school diplomas to students who are illiterate. Taken together, these factors have combined to spawn a nationwide trend emphasizing the much publicized back-to-basics movement.

One effect of these conditions is a demand for accountability in education—that is, a demand that educators be held responsible for what students learn. The call for accountability is not new,[3] but, given the ire of taxpayers facing inflationary times, it must be given more than superficial acknowledgment by educators in the 1980's. The response of many teacher training institutions to the previous cries for accountability was competency-based teacher education (CBTE). CBTE became *the* innovation in teacher training during the 1970's. CBTE is an approach to teacher training—

> . . . that focuses on students' acquisition of specific competencies. . . . Competencies are composite skills, behaviors, or knowledge that can be demonstrated by the learner.[4]

Hence, in CBTE programs, prospective teachers are held accountable for attaining specified levels of ability in performing essential teaching tasks. The essence of the programs is the identification of competencies that trainees must master in order to be certified.

Joining our colleagues in other areas, teacher educators in the field of speech communication advocated CBTE during the 1970's. In projecting about teacher preparation programs, Ratliffe suggested that "the essence of future models will probably be a focus upon competencies . . . essential to the teaching of communication. . . ."[5] In summarizing the implications of the 1973 Memphis Conference of Teacher Educators in Speech Communication, Friedrich offered CBTE as an "instructional strategy which holds great promise" as a creative and innovative approach to teacher education in speech communication.[6]

While literature on teacher education in speech communication during the 1970's contained statements advocating CBTE, reports describing the implementation of CBTE programs within the speech communication field have not been forthcoming.[7] One cannot help but infer, consequently, that perhaps few such programs have been implemented. Because many of the same conditions that fostered CBTE in the 1970's will exist in the 1980's, however, CBTE may still be the most appropriate way of responding to the challenge of training effective teachers. The remainder of this chapter presents a proposal for the implementation of a research-based, learner-sequenced, field-oriented CBTE program in speech communication designed to meet the needs of teacher education in the 1980's.

IDENTIFICATION OF COMPETENCIES

The foundation of successful CBTE rests on the identification of competencies that are essential to the teaching of speech communication and the organization of those competencies in a way that is meaningful to the trainees. For prospective elementary school language arts teachers and secondary school speech communication teachers, there are two important types of competencies: those dealing with the *content* of instruction and those dealing with the *process* of instruction.

Content-Oriented Competencies

Content competencies deal with what the speech communication teacher should teach. As Peters states: "If anything is to be regarded as a specific preparation for teaching, priority must be given to a thorough grounding in something to teach."[8] An indictment of teacher education that is continually being voiced is that training institutions turn out teachers who have studied methods of teaching but who are sorely lacking in the substance of what to teach.

During the late 1970's in the field of speech communication, strides were made toward generating content-oriented competencies. In the 1980's teacher educators do not have to rely upon their intuitions for curricular decisions; but can incorporate the findings of four research studies. Three were undertaken to determine the communication needs and abilities of students at various levels.[9] By means of surveys, literature reviews, and task force work, the authors derived and/or compiled competencies or objectives for K–12 students. It is essential not only that the teachers of our students be prepared to teach these skills, but also that they have mastered the skills. A fourth study offered competency guidelines to be achieved by speech communication specialists for K–12.[10]

The field of speech communication has expanded in recent years and has become more diverse. Teachers are no longer called upon merely to teach public speaking. Objectives from the questionnaire study of Cegala and Bassett, for example, included 13 categories of content with a broad range: listening, small group, processing information, nonverbal, problem solving, conflict, mass communication, feedback, public speaking, verbal expression, message analysis, personal growth, and interpersonal.[11] Speech communication teachers need to have more than a passing familiarity with the content of these areas; they need to have a thorough understanding of each. A synthesis of the competencies offered in these four sources would provide an important base in establishing the content that prospective speech communication teachers need to master.

Process-Oriented Competencies

The second important competency area for speech communication teachers is that dealing with the *process* of instruction. According to the

Speech Communication Association/American Theatre Association Task Force:

> . . . since teaching–learning processes are primarily symbolic interactions, teacher preparation programs should be concerned with . . . the development of the prospective teacher's own communication and performance competencies in order to facilitate learning. . . .[12]

Three different types of sources of such competencies are available. One source includes lists of communication competencies that have been generated through surveys[13] or by task force work.[14] A second source lists more general teacher competencies that have been compiled by education specialists, including communication competencies.[15] For example, competency categories such as relating interpersonally, interpersonal relationships, and interpersonal regard and group activity are clearly communication-related.

A third, and perhaps the most important, source is the findings of research efforts that have correlated communication-oriented variables (e.g., giving feedback) with student achievement. In a widely cited review of research on the relationship between teacher behavior and student learning, Rosenshine and Furst described nine variables that were most consistently related to student gain.[16] Seven of the nine can be considered communication variables: clarity, enthusiasm, use of structuring comments, task orientation, criticism, teacher indirectness, and use of multiple levels of questions or cognitive discourse. More recently, Medley synthesized a large number of studies that addressed this question: "How does the behavior of effective teachers differ from that of ineffective teachers?"[17] Many of the behaviors examined were communication behaviors (e.g., asks new question, repeats question, gives answer). Finally, Larson reviewed research that reported a significant relationship between teacher communication behaviors and student achievement (e.g., defining, paraphrasing).[18] Although these reviews isolated variables that were often general in nature, they can serve as a basis for competency statements. For example, from the variable of clarity, several competency statements can be generated: e.g., teacher gives students concise explanations of subject matter; teacher gives students concise directions that are readily understood without follow-up questions. An important task for teacher educators of the 1980's is to derive competencies from these research variables and then to synthesize them with competencies derived from sources previously mentioned. Such a synthesis would have the added advantage of having been generated by both classroom teachers and researchers.

ORGANIZATION OF COMPETENCIES

Learner-Sequenced Programs

Once competencies have been identified and selected for inclusion, it is necessary to organize them into an integrated program of teacher training. An important, yet often overlooked, factor in program planning is the relevance of the competencies to the prospective teachers. Hall and Jones propose that mastery of competencies is unlikely to occur unless the personal needs of the students are considered: "If a CBTE program actually ignores the personal psychosocial needs of students in the program, it is doomed."[19] They advocate a personalized program of teacher training that provides instruction that is sequenced according to the concerns of the prospective teachers.

Research has indicated that the general concerns and the communication concerns of prospective teachers can be conceptualized according to three phases: (1) concern about self as a teacher (adequacy and survival), (2) concern about the task of teaching (instructional duties), and (3) concern about impact (effect on pupil learning and pupil affect).[20] Concerns of teachers in training were found to differ from those of practicing teachers, with preservice teachers expressing more *self* and *task* concerns and in-service teachers expressing more *impact* concerns. The implication of this research for CBTE programs is that competencies should be sequenced according to the concerns of trainees in order for the program to be most meaningful to them. Such a learner-perceived sequence for presenting program competencies was advocated by Popham and Baker as early as 1970 when they stated that the interests and needs of the learner might well be one basis for curricular decisions. They reported on successful teachers who permitted a pupil's "areas of concern to help guide what is taught."[21] Hall and Jones suggest a similar approach in allowing prospective teachers to "acquire the skills and competencies they were concerned about or those that would help them alleviate their concerns when they needed to."[22]

For example, contrast two competencies, the first derived from a self concern and the second from an impact concern:

1. Presents self as a credible person whom students like and respect as a teacher.

2. Conveys to students a feeling that they are liked and respected.

While both of these are important competencies, research has demonstrated that self concerns are the most salient to prospective teachers. Thus, it is reasonable for trainees to achieve the first competency, then attempt the second. After mastery of the self competency, they will be more interested in attempting the impact competency.

Field-Oriented Programs

In addition to sequencing according to the concerns of prospective teachers, a final suggestion for improving CBTE programs in the 1980's is to shift the emphasis from classroom-oriented to field-oriented programs. Most teacher training programs include what is known as a student teaching or intern phase. Typically, this involves a short segment (one quarter or semester) of time spent in a school district under the supervision of a master teacher. The internship usually occurs at the end of the training period during the student's senior year.

Since many prospective teachers describe this aspect of their training as the most meaningful, it is reasonable that it should be the *basis* of our programs, not merely a one-time experience. As early as 1973 Ratliffe advocated "a shift of the student teaching experience from the periphery to the core of the teacher preparation model,"[23] but few descriptions of such programs in speech communication have been reported. In helping prospective teachers move through the phases of self, task, and impact concerns, a field-oriented program that extends over a longer period of time would allow them to resolve their concerns more effectively.[24] For example, competencies that deal with the area of self concerns would be addressed first in the training program. Students would take classes, study, and begin to master self-oriented competencies. They would then be given time in the school setting to practice and finally demonstrate mastery of competencies. In this way the field experience would extend over the duration of the training period and would more effectively prepare prospective teachers for their roles as practicing teachers.

CONCLUSION

Economic and societal trends affecting education at the onset of the 1980's are not vastly different from those during the mid and late 1970's. CBTE is still the most appropriate response to demands for accountability coupled with higher educational costs and an emphasis on basic skills. In CBTE programs, teachers would be certified only if they have demonstrated mastery of specified competencies determined to be crucial to the teaching of speech communication. By their mastery of both content and process competencies, prospective teachers would offer assurance that they are likely to be more effective than their peers who graduate from non-CBTE programs.

Three suggestions for improving CBTE in speech communication and for making it more effective in the 1980's have been offered in this chapter: (1) Both content and process competencies included in the CBTE programs should be based on research findings. (2) In order to make CBTE programs more relevant to trainees, competencies should be sequenced according to an empirically based, learner-perceived (concerns) sequence. (3) CBTE programs should decrease the emphasis on classwork and move to field-oriented approaches.

REFERENCES

1. Divoky, Diane. "Burden of the Seventies: The Management of Decline." *Phi Delta Kappan* 61: 87; October 1979.

2. Grant, W. Vance. "Statistic of the Month: Long-Range Trends in Public School Enrollment." *American Education* 14: 42; June 1978.

Ornstein, Allan C. "Teacher Surplus: Trends in Education's Supply and Demand." *Educational Horizons Journal* 57: 112; Spring 1979.

3. Welch, D.I. "The Quest for Accountability." *Journal of Teacher Education* 25: 59–64; 1974.

4. Hall, Gene E., and Jones, Howard L. *Competency-Based Education: A Process for the Improvement of Education.* Englewood Cliffs, N.J.: Prentice-Hall, 1976. p. 11.

5. Ratliffe, Sharon A. "Descriptions of Current Teacher Preparation Models and Possible New Models for Communication Education." Paper presented at the ninth annual summer conference of the Speech Communication Association, Chicago, July 1973.

6. Friedrich, Gustav W. "Implications for Speech Communication Teacher Education." *New Horizons for Teacher Education in Speech Communication.* (Edited by P. Judson Newcombe and R.R. Allen.) Skokie, Ill.: National Textbook Co., 1974. p. 169.

7. For a description of a performance-based program, which is similar to a competency-based one, see: Seiler, William J.; Cook, Gary; and DeSalvo, Vincent. "A Performance-Based Teacher Education Program in Speech and Drama." *The Speech Teacher* 24: 68–71; January 1975. For a general discussion of nationwide CBTE standards, see: Lynn, Elizabeth M. *Improving Classroom Communication: Speech Communication Instruction for Teachers.* Falls Church, Va.: Speech Communication Association, 1976. pp. 25–27.

8. Peters, R.S. *Education and the Education of Teachers.* London: Routledge and Kegan Paul, 1977. p. 151.

9. Brown, Kenneth L., and others. "A Summary of Communication Competencies Derived from the Literature Review." *Developing Communication Competence in Children.* (Edited by R.R. Allen and Kenneth L. Brown.) Skokie, Ill.: National Textbook Co., 1976. pp. 151–185.

Cegala, Donald J., and Bassett, Ronald E. "The Goals of Speech Communication Instruction: The Teacher's Perspective." *Developing Communication Competence in Children.* pp. 225–242, 259–272.

Bassett, Ronald E.; Whittington, Nilwon; and Staton-Spicer, Ann. "The Basics in Speaking and Listening for High School Graduates: What Should Be Assessed?" *Communication Education* 27: 293–303; November 1978.

10. SCA/ATA Joint Task Force on Teacher Preparation. "Competency Models in Speech Communication, Theatre and Mass Communication for Preparation and Certification of School Specialists and Non-Specialists." Report presented for approval to SCA and ATA, August 1976.

11. Cegala, Donald J., and Bassett, Ronald E. *op. cit.*

12. Joint Task Force of the SCA and ATA. "Guidelines for Speech Communication and Theatre Programs in Teacher Education." *The Speech Teacher* 24: 345; November 1975.

13. Staton, Ann Q. *An Empirical Investigation of the Communication Concerns of Preservice and Inservice Elementary School Teachers and an Identification of Competencies.* Doctoral dissertation. Austin: University of Texas, 1977.

Swinton, Marilyn M. *The Identification of Competencies Needed by Speech Communication/Drama Teachers with Implications for Use in Teacher Education Programs.* Master's thesis. Austin: University of Texas, 1979.

14. SCA/ATA Joint Task Force on Teacher Preparation. *op. cit.*

15. The author has identified 23 such competency lists. For complete citations, please write.

16. Rosenshine, Barak, and Furst, Norma. "Research in Teacher Performance Criteria." *Research in Teacher Education.* (Edited by B. Othanel Smith.) Englewood Cliffs, N.J.: Prentice-Hall, 1971. pp. 37–72.

17. Medley, Donald M. *Teacher Competence and Teacher Effectiveness.* Washington, D.C.: AACTE, 1977.

18. Larson, Kirby L. *Providing Theoretical Foundations for Effective Teacher Communication Behaviors.* Master's thesis. Seattle: University of Washington, 1979.

19. Hall, Gene E., and Jones, Howard L. *op. cit.* p. 136.

20. Fuller, Frances F. "Concerns of Teachers: A Developmental Conceptualization." *American Educational Research Journal* 2: 207–226; 1969.

Staton-Spicer, Ann Q., and Bassett, Ronald E. "Communication Concerns of Preservice and Inservice Elementary School Teachers." *Human Communication Research* 5: 138–146; Winter 1979.

21. Popham, William J., and Baker, Eva L. *Systematic Instruction.* Englewood Cliffs, N.J.: Prentice-Hall, 1970. p. 50.

22. Hall, Gene E., and Jones, Howard L. *op. cit.* p. 168.

23. Ratliffe, Sharon A. *op. cit.* p. 106.

24. For a brief description of a field-oriented elementary preservice teacher education program, see: Staton-Spicer, Ann Q.; Colson, Ella; and Bassett, Ronald E. "A Field-Oriented Teacher Education Program: Forum for Resolving Communication Concerns." *Social Education* 43: 378–380; May 1979.

Additional Readings

Anglin, Leo W.; Fox, G. Thomas, Jr.; and DeVault, M. Vere. "A Framework for Discussing Different Approaches to Teacher Education." ED 162 962. Paper presented at AERA, Toronto, March 1978. The authors present a framework for comparing teacher education programs by discussing assumptions about the variability of students and the nature of the instructional process. Four alternatives in teacher education programs are compared: traditional, interdisciplinary, open alternative, and competency-based.

Hall, Gene, and Jones, Howard L. *Competency-Based Education: A Process for the Improvement of Education.* Englewood Cliffs, N.J.: Prentice-Hall, 1976. This text provides a description of CBTE—what it is, how it came about, and how it can be implemented. The viewpoint presented is a practical one, and the text is an excellent introduction for newcomers to CBTE.

Lynn, Elizabeth M. *Improving Classroom Communication: Speech Communication Instruction for Teachers.* Falls Church, Va.: Speech Communication Association, 1976. This book reports the status nationally of instruction in speech communication for teachers. Included is a general discussion of nationwide CBTE standards.

Newcombe, P. Judson, and Allen, R.R. *New Horizons for Teacher Education in Speech Communication.* Skokie, Ill.: National Textbook Co., 1974. This book is a synthesis of the 1973 Memphis Conference on Teacher Education in Speech Communication. The current and future status of teacher education is discussed.

Speech Communication Association and American Theatre Association, Joint Task Force. "Guidelines for Speech Communication and Theatre Programs in Teacher Education." *The Speech Teacher* 24: 343–364; November 1975. This article is a description of competency guidelines for the preparation of specialists and nonspecialists in speech communication and theatre.

Staton-Spicer, Ann Q.; Colson, Ella; and Bassett, Ronald E. "A Field-Oriented Teacher Education Program: Forum for Resolving Communication Concerns." *Social Education* 43: 378–380; May 1979. The authors describe a field-oriented elementary education preservice teacher training program.

Molefi Kete Asante is Professor of Communication at The State University of New York—Buffalo. Among the books Dr. Asante has written are *Transracial Communication, Handbook of Intercultural Communication, Intercultural Communication: Theory into Practice* and *The Rhetoric of Black Revolution.*

Roy M. Berko is Professor of Communication at Lorain County Community College, Elyria, Ohio. Dr. Berko is the co-author of *Communicating: A Social and Career Focus* and *This Business of Communicating.* He is a past Chairperson of the Community College Section of the Speech Communication Association (SCA) and a member of its Educational Policies Board.

Cassandra L. Book is Associate Professor of Communication at Michigan State University. As director of the communication education program and of the basic communication course, Dr. Book has instructed communication teachers both at the university and in workshops across the country. Her publications include the secondary-level text *Person-to-Person: An Introduction to Speech Communication.*

Karlyn Kohrs Campbell is Professor of Speech and Drama at the University of Kansas. Dr. Campbell is the author of *Critiques of Contemporary Rhetoric* and the co-editor of *Form and Genre: Shaping Rhetorical Action.* She has served as a member of the SCA Research Board.

Pamela J. Cooper is Assistant Professor of Speech Education at Northwestern University. A former junior high and high school teacher, Dr. Cooper has written *Speech Communication for the Classroom Teacher.* In addition she has co-authored four books in speech communication.

John A. Daly is Assistant Professor in the Department of Speech Communication at the University of Texas. At the time of this writing, Dr. Daly is Chairperson of the Instructional Communication Division of the International Communication Association. He is also on the editorial boards of *Human Communication Research, Organizational Communication Abstracts,* and *Communication Education.*

172

Carolyn M. Del Polito is Director of Child Find and Advocacy for the American Society of Allied Health Professions; Dr. Del Polito was formerly the Director of Educational Services for the Speech Communication Association. She has authored *Intrapersonal Communication* and presented numerous papers and workshops at regional and national meetings of professional organizations.

B. Aubrey Fisher is Professor of Communication at the University of Utah. A former high school teacher, Professor Fisher is a member of the editorial boards of several professional journals. Among his publications are *Perspectives on Human Communication* and *Small Group Decision Making: Communication and the Group Process,* Second edition.

Mary Anne Fitzpatrick is Assistant Professor in the Department of Communication Arts at the University of Wisconsin—Madison. Her research interests currently focus on the study of communication in intimate, long-term relationships and family interaction processes. She has contributed articles to numerous professional journals.

Paul G. Friedman is Associate Professor of Speech Communication and Human Relations at the University of Kansas. A former secondary school teacher, Dr. Friedman's work has focused on communication in educational settings. Among his books are *Developing Children's Awareness Through Communication; Life-Shaping: A Guide to Creative Personal Change;* and *The A-Frame: Processes of Authentic Communication.*

Gustav W. Friedrich is Professor and Chair of the Department of Speech Communication at the University of Nebraska—Lincoln. He has co-authored *Teaching Speech Communication in the Secondary School, Public Communication,* and *Growing Together . . . Classroom Communication.* At the time of this writing, he is editor of *Communication Education* and president of the Central States Speech Association.

Kathleen M. Galvin is Chair of the Speech Education Department, School of Speech, Northwestern University. Dr. Galvin previously taught speech at Evanston Township High School and has run numerous communication workshops for secondary school teachers. She is the co-author of *Person to Person: An Introduction to Speech Communication* and *Growing Together . . . Classroom Communication.*

Bruce E. Gronbeck is Professor of Communication and Theatre Arts at the University of Iowa where he heads the Division of Rhetorical Studies. He is author or co-author of three basic public speaking textbooks —*The Articulate Person, Principles of Speech Communication,* and *Principles and Types of Speech Communication.*

Roderick P. Hart is Professor of Speech Communication at the University of Texas in Austin and specializes in the rhetorical analysis of public and interpersonal discourse. He is author of *The Political Pulpit* and co-author of *Public Communication.*

Lee Hudson is Guest Artist, Department of Theatre Arts, University of North Dakota. She has served on the faculty at the University of Texas at Austin, the University of Arizona, the University of Illinois, and the University of North Dakota. She edited *An Index to Studies in the Oral Interpretation of Literature: 1911–1975* and co-edited *A Directory of Teachers of Oral Interpretation,* and she co-authored *The Group Performance of Literature.*

Kathleen M. Hall Jamieson is Professor of Communication Arts at the University of Maryland—College Park.

Bonnie McD. Johnson is Associate Professor of Communication at the University of Oklahoma at Norman. She is the author of *Communication: The Process of Organizing.* She also has taught in the public schools and has conducted many training seminars and workshops.

James F. Klumpp is Associate Professor of Speech Communication at the University of Nebraska—Lincoln. Dr. Klumpp is co-author of *Public Policy Decision Making: Systems Analysis and Comparative Advantages Debate.* He is also on the editorial boards of *JAFA* and *Speaker and Gavel,* and is the Chair of the American Forensics Association Educational Practices Committee.

Barbara Lieb-Brilhart is on the staff of the National Institute of Education's Program on Dissemination and Improvement of Practice where her special interest includes communication processes in school improvement. Previously Dr. Lieb-Brilhart served as Associate Executive Secretary for Education and Research of the Speech Communication Association.

Beverly Whitaker Long is Professor and Chair of the Department of Speech Communication at the University of North Carolina at Chapel Hill. Formerly a secondary school teacher in Newport (Arkansas), she has also taught at the University of Texas at Austin, Northwestern University, DePauw University, and Southwest Texas State University. With Mary Frances Hopkins, she co-edited *Contemporary Speech.*

Peter V. Miller is Assistant Research Scientist, Survey Research Center, and Assistant Professor, Department of Communication, at The University of Michigan. He is a series editor (with James Carey of the University of Illinois) of the *Sage Annual Reviews of Communication Research* and a co-editor of one of those volumes, *Strategies for Communication Research.*

174

Ann Q. Staton-Spicer is Assistant Professor in the Department of Speech Communication at the University of Washington in Seattle. Dr. Staton-Spicer's teaching and research interests are in the area of instructional communication. In addition to teaching and research duties, she works with student interns in the teacher education program at the University of Washington.

Douglas M. Trank is Head of the Division of Communication Education and Professor of Rhetoric at the University of Iowa. A former secondary speech and English teacher, he also worked with the debate programs at the University of Utah and Old Dominion University. Dr. Trank is president of the Federation of Iowa Speech Organizations and board member/journal editor for Iowa Communication Association.

Andrew D. Wolvin is Director of the Speech Communication Division at the University of Maryland—College Park. A former secondary school teacher of speech and drama, Dr. Wolvin served as coordinator of the Speech Communication Education program at Maryland for several years. He is co-author of *This Business of Communication, Communicating: A Social and Career Focus,* and *Listening Instruction.*

Barbara S. Wood is Professor of Communication at the University of Illinois, Chicago Circle. Her text *Children and Communication: Verbal and Nonverbal Language Development* is in its second edition. Her approach to communication development is contained in two education monographs on *The Development of Functional Communication Competencies,* one for Pre-K–Grade 6 and another for Grades 7–12.